Suffer the Little Children:

The Lucy Letby Case Revisited

by Dr David Holding

First published in Great Britain in 2024 by
Words are Life
10 Chester Place,
Adlington, Chorley, PR6 9RP
wordsarelife@mail.com
www.wordsarelife.co.uk

Electronic version and paperback versions available for purchase on Amazon.
Copyright (c) Dr David Holding and Words are Life.

First edition 2024.

The right of Dr David Holding to be identified as the author of this work has been asserted by him in accordance with the Copyright, Design and Patents Act 1988.

All rights reserved. Without limiting the rights under copyright reserved above, no part of this publication may be reproduced, stored or introduced into a retrieval system, or transmitted, in any form or by any means (electronic, mechanical, photocopying, recording or otherwise), without the prior written permission of both the copyright owner and the publisher of this book. No paragraph of this publication may be reproduced, copied or transmitted save with written permission or in accordance with the provisions of the Copyright Act 1956 (as amended).

ABOUT THE AUTHOR

Dr David Holding studied history at Manchester University before entering the teaching profession in the 1970s. He taught in both state and independent sectors. During this time, he continued historical research culminating in both a Master's degree and a Doctorate. Having previously studied law, David gained a Master of Law degree in Medical Law, which enabled him to transfer to teaching legal courses at university. Since retiring, David has concentrated his research and writing on various aspects of local history, legal trials, forensic science and medico-legal topics.

ALSO BY DAVID HOLDING

Murder in the Heather: The Winter Hill Murder of 1838

This book is a unique account of a brutal murder that occurred on the summit of Winter Hill in Lancashire in 1838. The account draws on both contemporary media reports and court transcripts and examines the events leading to the killing of a 21-year-old packman. It details the trial proceedings of the only suspect in the case. The work concludes with a re-assessment of the case in the light of modern forensic investigation. The reader is invited to reach their own 'verdict' based on the evidence provided.

The Pendle Witch Trials of 1612

The book provides readers with a sequential overview of the famous chain of events that ultimately led to the execution of women accused of practising witchcraft in the county of Lancashire. It is presented as a chronological account of the famous trials at Lancaster Castle in 1612. This book introduces the evidence and interview transcripts that formed the major plank of the prosecution case and will appeal to both the general reader and local historian.

The Dark Figure: Crime in Victorian Bolton

This book provides an absorbing overview of crime in the Lancashire town of Bolton over the period 1850 to 1890. It is primarily based on documentary survey and analysis of court and police records covering the period. It assesses changes in crime over time and asks whether these relate to economic, social or political changes taking place at the same time. The reader is left to reflect on whether crime (in all its many forms) has changed over time.

Bleak Christmas: The Pretoria Colliery Disaster Of 1910

This work charts the events of the Lancashire Pretoria Pit disaster in December 1910. It reflects on the devastation it left to many local communities whose main source of employment was coal. The main sources analysed are the Home Office Report on the disaster and the Report of the Inquest. The findings of these detailed legal reports are presented in a format that will supplement existing material on the event. The book will also provide a reference source both for local historians and the interested general reader.

Doctors in The Dock: The Trials of Doctors Harold Shipman, John Bodkin Adams and Buck Ruxton

This book takes the reader on a journey into the world of three medical doctors in England, each coming from a different social background but with one common thread going through their lives. They all stood trial for murder. In each case, the reader is presented with all relevant evidence available to jurors in the case. The overall aim of this work is to invite readers to exercise their judgment in reaching a verdict.

The three books within this collection are also available individually:

The Last Temptation: The Trial of Dr Harold Shipman.

The Trial of Dr Buck Ruxton.

The Trial of Dr John Bodkin Adams.

Forensic Science Basics: Every Contact Leaves a Trace

This work is an absorbing introductory study of the techniques familiar from numerous trials, media reports and TV crime dramas. It begins with the basic principles of forensic science and then examines such aspects as the time of death, causes of death, weapons of crime, identification of offenders and much more. It provides essential reading for those who wish to gain a basic introduction to this fascinating area of science.

A Warning from History: The Influenza Pandemic Of 1918

The 1918 Influenza Pandemic was one of the most deadly events in human history, and understanding the events and experience of 1918 is of great importance to pandemic preparation. This book aims to address questions concerning the pandemic's origin, features and causes to provide the reader with an appreciation of the 1918 pandemic and its implications for future pandemics. This work caters to both the science-orientated and general reader in this crucial area of global and public health.

The Lady Chatterley Trial Revisited

The 1960 obscenity trial of Lady Chatterley's Lover remains a symbol of freedom of expression. It is also a seminal case in British literary and social history and is credited as the catalyst which encouraged frank discussion of sexual behaviour. This book introduces readers to the trial itself, describing the prosecution and defence opening and closing speeches to the jury and much more before culminating in the judge's summing-up and the final verdict. The reader is provided with all the evidence to reach a considered assessment of the case and a question to consider. Can certain literature 'actually' corrupt, or does it simply encourage expensive court trials and boost sales?

The Oscar Wilde Trials Revisited

It is only given to very few people to be the principal figure in three Old Bailey trials, before three different judges, and at three consecutive court sessions, all in one year. This complexity is one of the fascinations of the 1895 Oscar Wilde trials. In addition, they embodied celebrity, sex, humorous dialogue, outstanding displays of advocacy and political intrigue woven with issues of art and morality. Wilde's prosecution of the Marquess of Queensberry for criminal libel, and Wilde's later prosecution for 'gross indecency', reveal a complex person at odds with a class-centred and morally ambiguous Victorian society. This work considers these famous trials in chronological sequence and invites the reader to participate as an observer and potential juror in the proceedings. Finally, the reader is encouraged to consider the evidence presented at each trial and arrive at their own conclusions. This work will be of particular interest to law students owing to the counsel's skilfully demonstrated advocacy skills. It also caters for the general reader with a particular interest in presenting criminal cases in the courts in England.

The Whitechapel Murders of 1888

The killing of five women in the Whitechapel area of East London in 1888 remains the greatest and most horrendous of all unsolved murder mysteries. It is the classic cold case. This work takes a novel look into the case from the perspective of the criminal investigation itself. In this approach, the more speculative and conspiratorial theories surrounding the 'Jack the Ripper' crimes have been avoided. The reader is offered insights into these murders by employing the modern forensic techniques of geographical and offender profiling, which shed new light on these serial killings.

Forensic Pathology Basics: The Dead Do Tell a Story

In this work, the reader is taken on a sequential journey of discovery into the fascinating world of forensic pathology, with no previous knowledge of the subject being required of readers. Beginning with the initial discovery of a body, the reader experiences the processes involving the forensic pathologist from the initial examination and identification of the deceased to the final autopsy. The reader will be introduced to practical applications of the pathologist's skills and techniques at each stage. Past criminal cases will be introduced to demonstrate the variety of scenarios in which the assistance of the forensic pathologist is vital. The overall aim of this work is to provide the reader with a fascinating insight into the largely unseen involvement of the forensic pathologist in death investigations. It is especially fascinating when the circumstances involve criminal activity. The manner and causes of death are discussed in detail and cover the main areas of injury. A glossary of medical terminology is provided to explain the various terms used in the text. The work concludes with a selected bibliography to enable the reader to pursue their research in those areas they find particularly interesting and relevant.

The Coronavirus Pandemic: An English Perspective

The Coronavirus (COVID-19) pandemic of 2020 onwards has been described as the second most deadly event in recent human history. The first was attributed to the influenza pandemic of 1918. A comparison has been made between the two events because of the similarities regarding high mortality and because of the resultant impact the pandemics had on the social and economic structures of the countries involved. This work provides the reader with a comprehensive background to the virus's origins, its subsequent rapid spread in England, and the government's responses and control policies implemented to halt its progress. This work will be of interest to both the science-orientated and the general reader with concern in this vital area of public health and in the preparation for future pandemics.

Live Or Let Die? The Euthanasia Debate Revisited

Euthanasia is concerned with decisions relating to the 'end of life', and is a major focus for public, academic and legal debate. Emotional responses dominate and range from calls for more liberalisation to dire warnings that society has now embarked upon a 'slippery slope'. The legal and ethical issues which flow from the euthanasia debate encompass a wide range of matters which permeate medical law by questioning the respective roles of both the medical and legal professions. This work considers definitions of euthanasia, case studies and related law in the UK and Netherlands. This work emphasises the powerful struggle that exists in law, medicine and ethics regarding the nature, scope and foundations of the right to choose the manner of one's own death. Our thought-provoking conclusion considers: "Under what conditions, if any, is it permissible for patients and health professionals to intentionally end life?"

The Psychological Aspects of Eyewitness Evidence

Eyewitness evidence is typically given the most credibility in courts of law. However, it should be admitted with caution and a clear understanding that certain psychological factors can its reliability. This work invites the reader to consider these factors. Each chapter in the work considers the various stages involved in eyewitness testimony in courts of law, from the initial witnessing of an event, the questioning stage and culminating in the court trial itself, and the evidence's presentation. This work poses two questions for the reader to consider: "Exactly how reliable is eyewitness testimony?" and "What factors impact the accuracy of such evidence?"

Justice Delayed: Hillsborough Revisited

This work provides details of the official inquiries launched, post-Hillsborough, together with the new inquests and the criminal trials after. It is also an account of how the British establishment failed to deliver justice at every level and records a catalogue of failings in response to this major disaster. A 'grand scale' conspiracy went right to the top of the establishment and persisted because of collusion between the 'elites' in politics, police and media. But... the Hillsborough families prevailed against all the odds and retained their dignity in the face of great adversity. The reader is left to consider one vital question. "How did Parliament allow such injustice on this scale to remain for so long? The lasting lesson from this disaster is that there must never again, be any arbitrary time limit on justice and accountability.

Beyond Reasonable Doubt: The Jenkins Case Revisited

Most people will have heard of the murder of 13-year-old, Billie-Jo Jenkins in February 1997, in Hastings, East Sussex, and the discovery of her body by her foster father, Sion Jenkins. Everyone will have their own views as to what happened on that fateful day. This raises two pertinent questions. Where do we get our views from? And, what makes us think that we can possibly have any idea as to what actually happened? The chief suspect, Billie-Jo's foster father, Sion Jenkins, was subjected to a 'lynch mob' mentality, largely fuelled by the media and to seemingly endless legal processes. It became increasingly obvious that the police and some members of the judiciary, together with people that Jenkins considered friends (including his ex-wife) had a large part to play in what became a nightmare which Jenkins had to endure. This lasted from the day he discovered the body of Billie-Jo until he was finally acquitted, after having faced six years in prison, two appeals, and three criminal trials. This work exposes the deep failing of the criminal justice system. The deliberate tainting of the Jenkins children's evidence by the police, the failure by the police and CPS to disclose relevant information, together with attempts by the police at putting ideas into the head at Lois, Jenkins' ex-wife. Most people have faith in the criminal justice system, hence the saying 'mud sticks', because they cannot imagine that it can get it so wrong. Yet, the criminal justice system is damaged as is clearly demonstrated in this work. In this work, the reader is presented with the opportunity of experiencing a case which has become one of the greatest 'causes celebre' in British criminal history. The reader is invited to consider their own verdict based upon all the evidence presented to the juries in the three criminal trials. In arriving at their own conclusions, the reader will be able to balance the effects of ineptitude, confirmation bias, media 'hype', innuendo and misinformation, all of which were in plentiful supply in this case. This book brings into sharp focus the fact that it is unquestionably preferred to have all guilty people walk free than to have one innocent person in prison. At the heart of this case lies the truism that as soon as assumptions are made which are not supported by evidence, then the defendant in any criminal case faces an uphill struggle to obtain justice. Guilt must always be proven 'Beyond Reasonable Doubt'.

The Ukrainian Conflict: A British Perspective. Book One – The Year 2022

Book Two – The Year 2023

The Russian invasion of Ukraine in February 2022 is regarded as the greatest threat to the peace and security of Europe since the end of the Cold War. The objective of this work is to provide readers with an overview and assessment of the current conflict in Ukraine. To ensure a 'balanced' perspective, this work draws particular attention to the social, political, economic and military aspects of the war. The reader is presented with an analysis of the conflict on a month-by-month account based upon both media reporting and intelligence releases in both the US and the UK. The work includes a selection of commentaries written by military and political observers of the present Ukrainian conflict based on their own experiences. These are both personal and thought-provoking reflections. Their inclusion will provide the reader with an overview of the conflict and inform on the implications of the war for both the present and foreseeable future.

Acknowledgements

I am always grateful for the support and encouragement I receive during the course of my research. In particular, I wish to thank members of the legal, medical and scientific communities for the benefit of their opinions generously given, on the complex issues surrounding this particular case. My appreciation also extends to the staff at the various resource centres, archives and libraries I have consulted. My gratitude loses no sincerity in its generality.

No credits would be complete without special thanks and gratitude, to my ever-supportive and encouraging publisher and friend, Lesley Atherton. It is Lesley who provides the 'driving force' behind my work.

David Holding, 2024

Dr David Holding

Contents

Acknowledgements

Introduction 15

Chapter One: Suspicions 21

Chapter Two: Investigations 27

Chapter Three: The Trial 33

Chapter Four: The Aftermath 66

Chapter Five: Reflections 86

Epilogue 118

References And Bibliography 120

Dr David Holding

INTRODUCTION.

On 18 August 2023, neonatal nurse Lucy Letby was convicted of the murders of seven babies, and the attempted murder of a further six babies in the neonatal unit of the Countess of Chester NHS Trust hospital in Chester, where Letby was employed as a neonatal nurse.

This work examines the events at the hospital involving Lucy Letby and covers the period from June 2015 until June 2016. This involves an analysis of the initial suspicions regarding the sudden deaths and collapses of babies, internal reviews and the police investigation, culminating in Letby's trial at Manchester Crown Court in October, 2022.

In 2015, several reports were made by clinical staff concerning the increase in the numbers of baby deaths and non-fatal collapses in the neonatal unit. It appears that these concerns raised by clinical staff were initially ignored or dismissed by senior management at the time. Observers of the case have attributed this to a 'power imbalance' existing between the hospital's clinical staff and senior management. Once Lucy Letby had been assigned to work in the neonatal unit, a series of baby deaths and collapses occurred in regular succession over the 12-month period from 2015 to 2016. Following each of these events, it seems that initially, clinical staff, though considering these deaths as 'unusual and unexpected', believed they could be explained on the basis of each baby's medical history.

However, as more premature babies died or collapsed unexpectedly, the medical staff were then faced with a dilemma of serious proportions. Over the twelve-month period, it became clear that someone was 'deliberately' harming the babies in the unit. After initial reluctance by senior hospital management, the police were informed of the concerns and a criminal investigation was commenced in May 2017.

This investigation eventually resulted in the identification of Lucy Letby as the 'prime suspect'. She was arrested in July 2018 and in November 2020, was charged with 8 counts of murder and 10 of attempted murder, and was remanded in custody to await trial. On 10 October 2022, Lucy Letby stood trial at Manchester Crown Court. On 18 August 2023, Letby was found guilty of 14 of the 22 charges brought against her. On 21 August 2023, she was sentenced to life imprisonment with a whole-life order. The complexity of the Letby case and the recent denial of leave for her to appeal her convictions highlights the pivotal role that scientific evidence played in the Letby trial. This denial clearly indicates the uphill struggle through a legal system where evidence can exonerate but also condemn. What lies at the centre of the Letby trial is the reliability of the scientific evidence presented to the jury.

At Letby's trial, the evidence presented to the jury comprised medical records, text messages and personal handwritten jottings. It has been suggested that all these were submitted by the prosecution to form a chain of guilt with which to snare Letby. It is of particular significance that this evidence was not presented in a pure form, but instead was subject to 'interpretation, expert opinion, and contested reliability'. When Letby's trial is analysed, it indicates that her defence was questionable, not only in terms of its presentation, but also for the experts they chose or failed to choose, to challenge the prosecution's case. It has been suggested that the 'reliability of the scientific interpretation' of the evidence should have been challenged more robustly. The absence of this resulted in the court, and more specifically, the jury, being left to ponder the reliability of expert opinion, the veracity of amended medical records and the implications to be drawn from

Letby's personal diaries and jottings.

There is little doubt that the trial represented a scenario in which the science was as much on trial as Letby herself. By implication, the reliance on expert testimony is by its very nature, subject to 'personal interpretations and biases'. These can and do, influence a jury's perceptions of the case.

Furthermore, with this reliance on subjective interpretation, and where definitive scientific consensus is absent, how does one (or a jury), distinguish between evidence and inference, and fact or fiction? Some commentators of Letby's trial have gone so far as to suggest that it was a show trial with Letby being a scapegoat.

Letby's crimes were committed between June 2015 and June 2016 and have given the impression that an exceptional number of babies died during that time period. However, there were also other contributory factors not related to nursing care arising during this same period. Of particular significance here, is that the peak of infant mortality at the neonatal unit occurred in 2019, after Letby had left the hospital.

Critical to the guilty verdict was the chart of shift data displaying which nurses were on duty in the unit at the material time of the baby deaths and collapses. On the surface, this data is convincing, since Letby was present on all of these occasions. However, this evidence, taken in isolation, was misleading. Evidence has emerged that other casualties occurred when Letby was, in fact, off duty at the time. These facts were not even considered during the course of the trial. Data obtained from a Freedom of Information request to the Chester hospital, confirms that during the 12-months of Letby's crimes, 31 infants died, yet 23 of these were excluded from the trial. This would strongly suggest that Lucy Letby was being implicated by circular logic. Deaths and collapses happened when she was working on the unit, therefore, she must be guilty of causing harm.

It was widely reported that hospital doctors on the neonatal unit contended that the senior hospital management did not respond to the doctors' concerns regarding Letby. However, the management did respond by ordering three independent reviews regarding these concerns. However, the conclusions reached by the reviews proved rather negative, stating that neither Letby nor any other individual was to blame for the events. It was only when Letby insisted on apologies from the doctors concerned, indicating that she was prepared to make a formal complaint to the General Medical Council, that the doctors decided to involve police in the matter.

Since Letby was working in the unit when the baby deaths occurred, this suggested to investigators that there was a pattern of suspicious activity. However, patterns, coincidences and statistical blips can and do happen without any reason for them being found.

Analysis of Letby's trial strongly suggests that it was based entirely upon circumstantial evidence. Yet it, together with medical witnesses' theories and memories, were treated as hard evidence. Post-mortems for each of the babies who died were carried out, but the reports from these were never presented at the trial. Instead, these were replaced with the personal views of two experts, each with their own fresh conclusions as to the cause of death in each case.

Parallels have been drawn between the Letby crimes and those perpetrated by nurse Beverly Allitt back in 1991. At her trial and subsequent public inquiry, it was shown that Allitt, like Letby, was a nurse in her 20s at the time the crimes were committed. It was concluded that Allitt harmed her victims to win the sympathy and approval of others. Similarly, it has been suggested that Lucy Letby appeared to enjoy the attention she received when babies in her care collapsed.

In his closing address to the jury, Nicholas Johnson KC, prosecuting, described Lucy Letby as a "cold-blooded and calculating murderer who gas-lighted her colleagues into believing the deaths of the premature babies were a stroke of bad luck". She got away with her campaign of violence because hospital staff did not contemplate the remotest possibility of a nurse trying to kill tiny babies.

In his closing address to the jury, Letby's defence counsel, Ben Myers KC, informed the jury that the case against Lucy Letby was "fuelled by the presumption of guilt". The prosecution had "twisted and changed their theory to fit claims that Letby had killed and harmed the babes in her care". Mr Myers maintained that the post-it notes and jottings discovered during the police search of her home, were not a confession but expressions of fear and despair on being accused of killing newborns. He told the jury that there was no evidence proving Letby had engaged in the acts of murder or attempted murder. The whole case against her had been constructed solely upon assumptions and coincidences. The fact that Letby had been present at the time of the deterioration of a baby became the explanation for that deterioration, even without hard evidence.

This work concludes by presenting the reader with two questions to consider, having completed a journey of discovery into this tragic yet memorable case.

What turned this young, dedicated neonatal nurse into a cold, calculating and relentless baby killer?

How was she able to carry out these unthinkable murders within the confines of a hospital dedicated to saving the most vulnerable of patients?

There is now in progress, a public inquiry (Thirlwall Inquiry) into the Letby case, which will investigate all the areas of concern highlighted in this case. According to an article in *The Guardian*:

"We need the Inquiry to thoroughly examine NHS leadership, accountability and culture, to contextualise what happened. Among the many questions the Inquiry will need to answer and without prejudice, is 'Why did the leadership of this Trust act in the way they did?' Related to that: 'Why do leaders in the wider NHS too often act in a way that prioritises protecting the reputation of their organisation, over patient safety?' NHS leaders and ministers should make the difficult decisions to take a 'wide-angle lens approach' to this case, and use the sadness of this tragedy to make a step-change to the culture and values of the NHS, and ensure openness and transparency are really embedded at every level, from Ward to Board".

Source: The Guardian, 15, September, 2023.
Author: Denis Campbell, Health Policy Editor.

It is sincerely hoped by all concerned parties, that this Inquiry will provide the families of Lucy Letby's victims, with the answers they so desperately need and deserve.

CHAPTER ONE

Suspicions

Lucy Letby was born on 4th January 1990, in Hereford, the only child of John, a former shop manager and Susan, a retired accounts clerk. Lucy was educated at the Aylestone Comprehensive School before continuing her studies at Hereford Sixth Form College. She secured a place on a three-year degree course in Child Nursing at the University of Chester, graduating in 2011 with a BSc degree in Child Nursing. While her parents were unhappy about her moving away from Hereford to Chester, they did help her to buy her first home, a three-bedroom, semi-detached house near to the university. She lived there alone with two rescue cats. While studying, she worked as a student-nurse on placements at Liverpool Women's Hospital, and the Countess of Chester Hospital.

Letby began her career as a registered nurse on the neonatal unit at the Chester Hospital in 2012. In a staff profile of 2013, Letby had stated that she was responsible for "caring for a wide range of babies requiring various levels of support, and that she enjoyed seeing them progress, and supporting their families". She also took part in a campaign to raise funds for a new neonatal unit at the hospital. It was also noted that Letby chatted about her life and that she was single and happy being so.

Suspicious Cases

The first suspicious case occurred on 8 June 2015. At 8:00 pm, a healthy baby boy, a twin, was being cared for in Nursery 2 in the unit, the designated nurse being Lucy Letby. The boy had been handed over to Letby when she commenced her night shift. The paediatric registrar on duty had clocked off when Letby was 30 minutes into her shift, t about 8:30 pm. Around 8:55 pm, Letby called for a doctor when this baby's condition began to rapidly deteriorate. The baby died 30 minutes later, at approximately 9:26 pm. The registrar reported later that when she heard about the death of the child the next day, it was a "total surprise and completely out of the blue and upsetting".

This baby had showed no signs of any problems during the day. The registrar remarked that she had no concerns at all for him or his twin sister. Another nurse said that when the baby started to deteriorate, she saw Letby standing over the baby's incubator but did not intervene at first. When she did realise that the baby was not recovering under Letby's care, she did intervene and summoned the doctors. When they attended the scene, they saw that Child A had developed an unusual blue and white colouring on his skin after collapsing. They admitted that they had never experienced this before. It is significant that these same symptoms appeared later in other babies.

On 9 June 2015, 28 hours after Child A's death, his twin sister Child B inexplicably collapsed and had to be resuscitated. After Child A's death, his parents had spent the day with Child B in the nursery. However, they were persuaded to go and rest before this baby's sudden crash. Tests later revealed 'loops of gas-filled bowel' in the child. It was later concluded that the baby had been injected with air. It transpired that Letby had fed the baby 25 minutes before her collapse. The child had the same unusual skin rash as seen on her brother (Child A) earlier, indicating that she too, had been injected with air.

On 14 June 2015, Child C, a boy in a stable condition sadly died. He suddenly collapsed as the nurse supervising for him left the nursery for a short time before returning. Not being the child's designated nurse, Letby was witnessed standing over his monitor as his alarm sounded when the other nurse returned to the nursery. It appears that Letby's shift leader had told her repeatedly to focus on her designated patient. This shift leader testified that she had pulled Letby away from the family room in which Child C died.

On 22 June 2015, a baby girl, Child D, collapsed in the early hours and died. Those attempting to save the child noticed the girl's skin was also discoloured. A post-mortem x-ray showed a 'lined gas' in front of her spine, consistent with air being injected into her bloodstream. A doctor later testified that such a finding could not be explained by natural causes. The girl's mother had noted Letby 'hanging around' the family before the baby collapsed. On 2 July 2015, a doctor raised his concerns over the sudden collapses and deaths of these babies. No action was taken against Letby at this point in time.

These suspicious cases stopped for about one month. However, at around 9:00 pm on 3 August 2015, the mother of Child E had come to the neonatal unit to give him and twin Child F her expressed breast milk. She became alarmed by a scream coming from the room of Child E. She discovered the child with fresh blood around his mouth and in extreme distress. Letby, who was standing next to his incubator, explained that the bleeding had been caused by a feeding tube rubbing in his mouth. Child E died in the early hours of 4 August 2015. He had lost around 25% of his total blood volume. 'Injected air' was suspected as being the cause of his death. Unfortunately, no post-mortem was carried out on this baby.

In the evening of 4 August, Child E's twin brother, Child F, was being cared for in Nursery 2, the same room in which Letby was looking after another baby. At 1:54 am, Child F suffered an unexpected drop in his blood-sugar levels, and a surge occurred in his heart rate. Fortunately, the child survived and a later blood test revealed that he had been given an 'extremely high amount' of exogenous insulin, which he did not require. No baby on the unit had been prescribed insulin at any time. There was no reason why Child F should have been given insulin.

On 7 September 2015, Child G collapsed on three occasions over the course of three weeks. This baby had been alive for 100 days. After the first collapse, this baby girl was transferred to Arrowe Park Hospital on the Wirral for special care. She then returned to the Chester neonatal unit.

Five days later, the baby collapsed after Letby had been feeding her. This child did survive but is now severely disabled. Her heart rate and oxygen levels had dropped to 'unusually low levels'. According to an expert medical witness, the only viable explanation was that this baby had received far more milk than was allocated down her nasogastric feeding tube. This could not have occurred accidentally. A nurse observed that when she arrived after Letby raised the alarm for help following one of the baby girl's collapses, the machine connected to monitor her oxygen saturation and heart rates had been switched off.

About six weeks after Child G's multiple collapses, on 23 October 2015, Child I died. This was the fourth time this baby had collapsed. On this collapse, Letby was found by another nurse next to the child's incubator. Twice this baby was found to have excess air in her stomach which had affected her breathing. Before the second collapse, Letby told a colleague that Child I 'looked pale', even though it was hard to see from where they were standing in a doorway looking into a 'darkened nursery room'. When the designated nurse for this child turned the light on, she saw that the baby girl was not breathing.

The child's mother later said Letby 'smiled' as she bathed her dead daughter.

A doctor had noticed the unusual skin colour on Child I. X-rays revealed that the child had a' massively enlarged stomach' that was consistent with her having been deliberately injected with air.

By April 2016, Letby had been moved to day shifts because of growing concerns about her, Then, suspicious collapses began occurring again in the daytime.

On 9 April 2016, twin brothers suffered sudden collapses within hours of each other. Tests revealed that Child L had insulin levels in his blood at the very top of the scale that any available equipment was capable of measuring. Hours later, his twin brother, Child M's, heart rate and breathing suddenly dropped and he nearly died. Experts expressed that Child M's heart-rate decrease was likely to have been caused by air injected into his bloodstream. Although this baby did survive, he now suffers from brain damage.

It was noted that the collapse of Child L and Child M occurred in almost identical circumstances to Child E and Child F. Both of these were twins, where one was believed to have been injected with insulin and the other with air.

Child F had survived his injection of insulin. It was noted that Child L had been injected with twice the dose of insulin. A meeting about the suspicious cases took place on 11 May 2016, but no action was taken by management.

A month later, Child N almost died after suffering trauma to his throat. Doctors saw blood and unusual swelling at the back of his throat. The baby had been heard screaming. The child's father said he saw blood spattered around his son's mouth.

The final two cases occurred within hours of each other on 23 and 24 June, 2016. The two babies involved were triplets, siblings of each other. These cases occurred on Letby's first shift after a holiday abroad. Child O, a 'perfect' healthy baby, was due to be discharged home but suddenly collapsed on 23 June.

When the child initially became unwell, another nurse suggested he be moved to Nursery 1, where the sickest children were treated, but Letby disagreed. Less than two hours later, the baby subsequently collapsed. He recovered but suffered two further collapses and died almost three hours later. The lead consultant noted that the child should have responded better to resuscitation. X-rays on a post-mortem revealed he had an abnormal amount of gas in his body, together with liver damage. An independent pathologist later ruled that this had resulted from an 'impact injury'. He likened this to being similar to that with impact in a vehicle crash.

Fifteen minutes after Child O's death, Letby was feeding his triplet brother, Child P, who was expected to be able to go home, but collapsed after his diaphragm was found to be shattered. However, doctors believed that he would make a full recovery. As they prepared him to go to another hospital in the area, Letby said: "He's not leaving here alive, is he?" The boy died soon afterwards.

X-rays likewise showed an inexplicable amount of gas inside the baby. These deaths were described as 'exceptional' and the 'tipping point'. The consultants realised that drastic action needed to be taken. A consultant allowed the surviving triplet to be taken to a different hospital by medics who had arrived to take Child O. This consultant said she allowed this after her parents begged for it, as she now felt Letby was a 'moral danger' to the surviving triplet, Child P. Shortly afterwards, Child P collapsed and died.

Towards the end of June 2016, Letby was removed from the neonatal unit to a clerical role within the hospital. The suspicious collapses suddenly ceased.

CHAPTER TWO
Investigations

An informal review into the series of adverse events at the Countess of Chester Hospital was commenced in June 2015, by lead consultant and neonatologist Dr Stephen Brearey. This initially revealed details concerning four unexplained collapses on the neonatal unit at the hospital. Three of these had resulted in the deaths of Child A, C and D, all having occurred during the same month. It was observed that Lucy Letby had been on duty on each of these occasions.

The unit's consultants reported these three deaths to the Hospital trust's committee responsible for addressing serious incidents. This resulted in the committee regarding the three deaths as 'Medication Errors'. The general feeling among the nursing and medical staff was that since thy had been classified as 'serious incidents' resulting in 'unexpected deaths' then an immediate investigation should have been launched.

The numbers of unexplained collapses were without doubt, abnormal. Prior to these events, there had been at most, two or three deaths each year in the neonatal unit. The most unusual aspect of these babies' deaths, was that they did not respond to resuscitation attempts as would be expected in these cases. Normally, babies that got a heart beat back would see an improvement in their breathing ability, but in these particular cases, this did not occur.

Detective Superintendent Paul Hughes of Cheshire Constabulary CID, who would later lead the criminal investigation, was informed by two consultants that baby collapses which occurred during the 'spike' of incidents, had been totally unexpected, and as such, could not be explained. Both of these aspects were not usual with infant collapses generally.

Then in October 2015, the nursing manager for the unit conducted her own review and particularly noted that Letby was the only staff member who was 'consistently present' throughout these incidents of unexplained collapses and deaths. Her findings were reported to the lead consultant and neonatologist. These concerns were expressed to the hospital management by the unit's consultants which resulted in them either being resisted by the trust's executives or simply ignored. In February 2016, the lead neonatologist together with other consultant colleagues, concluded another review investigating five unexplained deaths and collapses within the unit. Together, these 'staff initiated' reviews led to the conclusion that the only 'common factor' in all these cases was the 'presence of Lucy Letby'. The lead consultant communicated these 'disturbing findings' up to the trust's Medical Director. This did result in a meeting with the executive team later in 2016.

However, the events were deemed to be 'coincidental' and resulted in no positive action being taken by the executives. A review carried out by the 'Mothers and Babies: Reducing Risk through Audits and Confidential Enquiries across the UK' (MBRRACE) did find a neonatal death rate which was at least 10% higher than what should have been expected in the period between June 2015 and June 2016. The neonatal death total in 2015 had doubled to that of 2014. It was concluded that the mortality rate in the neonatal unit at the Countess of Chester Hospital had certainly risen above normal rate. During a hospital visit by the Care Quality Commission (CQC) in February 2016, it was informed of difficulties in raising concerns with managers. However, it does appear that they did not hear any mention of an 'elevated mortality rate'. The CQC's report identified issues of staffing in the unit. Surprisingly, it praised "positive culture where staff felt well supported, were able to raise concerns and develop professionally".

On June 24 2016, following the further deaths of two triplet babies on that day and the previous one, the lead neonatologist phoned the Duty Executive to demand that Lucy Letby be 'removed from the unit altogether'. It appears that this executive insisted that Letby was 'safe to work' and that she (the executive) was 'happy to take responsibility' if anything happened to any more babies under Letby's care. In late June 2016, the trust's Executive Directors convened to address the question of 'whether to involve law enforcement'. By this time, seven unexpected deaths had occurred within the neonatal unit. The unanimous view among the hospital's executives was that the indicators of Letby's involvement were largely circumstantial. They also suggested that certain doctors had embarked on a 'misguided witch-hunt'.

They were particularly concerned about the potential harm to the Trust's reputation which could result from a police inquiry. As a result, they ultimately opted against involving the police. Instead, the Medical Director and Chief Executive arranged for a further review to be undertaken through the Royal College of Paediatrics and Child Health (RCPCH). This began in September 2016. It also appears that in July 2016, the unit's services were 'scaled back'. This in effect, meant that the neonatal unit at Chester no longer treated premature births before the 32-week mark. These cases would be transferred to other hospitals in the North-West, the closest to Chester being Alder Hey Children's Hospital in Liverpool.

It would appear that the Trust has set a 'narrow scope' for the review that totally excluded investigating Letby's actions or the increased deaths. Instead, it focused on the unit's general service. The RCPCH reported their findings back to the Medical Director and Chief Executive in October 2016. Even they could not find a definitive explanation for the increase in the mortality rate at the unit. However, they found some insufficient staffing and senior cover. More importantly, the report recommended a 'detailed case review' of each of the unexplained deaths.

The Medical Director approached neonatologist Dr Jane Howdon from Great Ormond Street Hospital in London, to carry out this case review. Howdon responded that she could not conduct a detailed review due to lack of time. However, she could provide a summary. This would be based on her reviewing the relevant medical notes and records. She did identify four cases that would 'potentially benefit from local forensic review as to circumstances, personnel etc'.

The board's chairman at the time complained that he had been misled about the scope of that review and its findings. Despite the thorough external independent review recommended by the RCPCH or the forensic review recommended by Jane Howdon, records of this hospital board meeting show that the Medical Director told the board members that the RCPCH and Howdon reviews concluded that the deaths in the neonatal unit were due to "issues with leadership and timely intervention".

In September 2016, Letby raised a formal grievance about her late June 2016 transfer from clinical duties to the hospital's 'risk and patient safety office'. Her grievance was upheld by the board in January 2017. They determined that her removal had been orchestrated by the consultants with 'no hard evidence'. They even supported her return to the neonatal unit and offered her a placement at the regional Alder Hey Children's Hospital in Liverpool. The Medical Director commented in his report that the trust's intention "was to protect Lucy Letby from these allegations".

The trust's Chief Executive had met with Letby and her parents on 22 December 2016. He apologised on behalf of the trust and gave then assurance that the doctors who made the allegations would be dealt with. In fact, he later ordered the consultants to send a letter of apology to Letby, which they reluctantly did in February 2017.

In March 2017, consultants asked the trust's management to involve the police after receiving advice from the regional neonatal lead, who suggested further investigation was required. They met with Cheshire Constabulary on 27 April 2017 to raise concerns that Letby was due to return to work on 3 May 2017.

The trust announced the involvement of the police in May 2017, stating that this move was to seek assurances that enable us to rule out 'unnatural' causes of death. The police investigation was code-named 'Operation Hummingbird'. The appointed Senior Investigating Officer (SIO), Detective Superintendent Paul Hughes, stated: "the initial focus was around the hypotheses of what could have occurred. The general hypotheses of it could be natural-occurring collapses, it could be organic reasons. it could be a virus, and it could be inflicted harm".

On 3 July 2018, Letby was arrested on suspicion of eight counts of murder and six counts of attempted murder following a year-long police investigation.

After Letby's arrest, the investigation was widened to include Liverpool Women's Hospital, another location where Letby did her training as a student-nurse.

Letby was bailed on 6 July 2018 as the police inquiry continued. Letby was re-arrested on 10 June 2019 on suspicion of eight cases of murder and nine cases of attempted murder, and released once more on bail on 13 June 2019. This was followed by another arrest on 10 November 2020. She was then charged with eight counts of murder and ten counts of attempted murder.

On this last occasion, Letby was denied bail and remanded in custody to await trial. The Crown Prosecution Service (CPS) were by this stage convinced to approve all of the charges requested by Cheshire Constabulary after it reviewed all the evidence the force had gathered against

Letby. She denied all 22 charges against her, blaming the deaths on 'hospital hygiene and insufficient staffing in the unit'. On 11 March 2020, Letby was placed on an interim suspension by the Nursing and Midwifery Council. This was followed up on 18 August 2023, when the Council commenced the necessary steps to strike Letby off the register.

CHAPTER THREE
The Trial

The King
v
Lucy Letby

Before
The Honourable Mr Justice Goss KT.
Manchester Crown Court.

Counsel for the Prosecution:
Nicholas Johnson KC.

Counsel for the Defence:
Ben Myers, KC.

The trial began on 10 October 2022, before Mr Justice Goss at Manchester Crown Court. Letby pleaded not guilty to seven counts of murder and 15 counts of attempted murder, totalling 22 counts. The child victims were referred to as Child A to Child Q. In 2020, Mrs Justice Steyn banned the identification of the living victims until they reached their 18th birthday. In addition, parents wanted their identifying information to be protected, including several witnesses who requested similar anonymity. The judge approved these requests.

Opening for the prosecution, Mr Nicholas Johnson, KC, said that Letby either poisoned the babies with insulin, injected air into their bloodstreams and stomachs, or overfed them with milk. The court was told that one child who was allegedly targeted by Letby, was delivered at 23 weeks, weighing only 1 lb 2oz at birth. However, despite her prematurity, Child G had been making good progress.

However, she suffered irreversible brain damage resulting in severe disability. This was the result of allegedly being injected three times with milk and air by Letby over a period of two weeks in September, 2015.

The court was told that Child G was permanently harmed a month after the death of the fourth alleged murder victim – Child E, a twin boy – when Letby was caught attacking him by his mother during a night shift. The mother was visiting the neonatal unit to deliver breast milk to her seven-day old son, who was due a feed at 9:00 pm. Mr Johnson said that she discovered Letby with the infant who appeared acutely distressed and was bleeding from his mouth in his incubator. The court was told that Letby reassured the mother that the bleeding had been caused by the nasogastric tube that was irritating his throat. Mr Johnson said that Letby urged the mother to return to the labour ward where she was being treated after having a Caesarean section birth. He further added that Letby told the mother: "Trust me, I'm a nurse" when in reality, she was in the course of attacking the baby at the time.

The boy's mother stated that, after discovering Letby with her son in distress at 9:00 pm, she phoned her husband from the labour ward. Phone records showed this call was made at 9:11 pm. By 11:40 pm, Child E had begun to collapse. He developed a purple and white rash and was bleeding during resuscitation attempts. Despite these attempts by medical staff, Child E was pronounced dead two hours later. His mother, father and Letby were all present at the baby's death. The on-duty medical registrar stated that he had never seen such a 'huge' bleed in a small baby, weighing just under 3 lbs. Experts later equated this blood loss to be around 25% of the total blood volume in his body. The registrar commented that Child E's rash reminded him of what he had observed during the death of Child A, the first baby alleged to have been killed by Letby, who died two months earlier.

The Court heard that Child E's death was initially put down to 'necrotising enterocolitis', a serious disorder common in premature infants which causes the bowel to become inflamed and die. Mr Johnson said that no post-mortem was carried out on Child E which, with hindsight, was a 'big mistake'.

Experts who later examined Child E's medical notes disagreed that 'enterocolitis' was to blame, and concluded that this baby died because 'air had been deliberately injected' into his bloodstream. This had caused a 'embolus' or bubble, which can block the flow of blood to the heart and other major organs. Another expert, Dr Dewi Evans, stated that the bleeding was 'indicative of trauma' but the unfortunate absence of a post-mortem examination meant that it was impossible to confirm what exactly had caused it. Mr Johnson said that Letby had failed to mention the blood around Child E's mouth witnessed by his mother, when she came to write up his medical notes after his death. She had also altered the timings of her visit to 'cover her tracks'.

The jury was told that Child E was the fourth infant who had died in the neonatal unit between June and August, 2015. Mr Johnson said that his twin brother, Child F, had been targeted by Letby, who had deliberately injected insulin into his feed the following day, but he survived. The prosecution did not dispute the fact that Child F had been poisoned with insulin and that Letby was responsible.

Mr Johnson described Letby as a 'malevolent and constant presence' at the neonatal unit when 17 babies had collapsed or died. He had previously informed the jury that doctors at the hospital were 'baffled by the increased mortality rate' at the unit and could not attribute a medical cause. However, the presence of Letby was the one 'common denominator'.

The court heard that a note discovered by police at Letby's home when she was arrested in July 2018, stated:

"I don't deserve to live. I killed them on purpose because I'm not good enough. I am a horrible, evil person. I am evil. I did this". Many other random words and phrases including "panic, fear and lost" were written in capital letters. The word 'hate' had been written and circled in black ink on a coloured notelet. On another piece of paper, Letby had written: "I haven't done anything wrong. Why has this happened? And they have no evidence, so why have I had to hide away?"

Nicholas Johnson, prosecuting, said several handwritten notes were recovered by police, together with medical documents relating to 17 babies that Letby was accused of murdering and injuring. Confidential paperwork concerning other babies she cared for was also found at her home. When interviewed by police, she denied keeping them as souvenirs.

Ben Myers KC, Letby's defence counsel, said that in Letby's case the 'post it note' was not a confession but an anguished outpouring of a young woman in fear and despair. She wrote it after learning that she was being accused of killing the new born babies, she had 'done her best' to look after.

Mr Myers added: "What you see there is anguish not guilt". Mr Myers told the jury that Letby was 'dedicated and loved her job'. She "cared deeply about the babies and in no way did she want to harm them". Mr Myers continued telling the jury that there was no evidence that showed Letby engaged in the act of murder or attempted murder. He suggested that the case against her had been constructed solely upon "assumptions and coincidences". He continued: "The fact that Lucy Letby has been present at the time of the deterioration of a child has itself, become the explanation of that deterioration, even though there is no evidence to show she has caused that to happen". Mr Myers said many of the babies at the unit were on the 'cliff edge of life', with all except one being born prematurely, together with very low birth weights. He said they were clinically fragile, and at a risk of rapid and unexpected deterioration. Sometimes there was no clear medical explanation for their collapse in health. He said identifying problems in such infants required both doctors and nurses watching, recording and communicating, but this proved difficult in a unit that was "understaffed and overstretched".

Mr Myers further pointed out that in July 2016, one month after the final alleged victim died, the neonatal unit at Chester was redesignated from a level two unit capable of caring for babies born after 27 weeks, to a level one unit which only cared for infants born after 32 weeks. Mr Myers added: "There is a question of whether this hospital should have been caring for all these infants, and whether it did so to the required standard".

Mr Myers said that this case hinged on the medical evidence. He then went through each of the 22 allegations against Letby, stressing that Letby was adamant she had not intentionally caused any of the babies' harm.

Mr Myers told the court that defence experts would dispute the cause of death. Some of the babies in the unit received what he termed sub-optimal care, while others weighed 2 lbs or less. These should, according to Mr Myers, have been in 'specialised centres.' Mr Myers told jurors that it was important that "blame is not heaped on Letby when there may be others who have made mistakes, or a system that has failed". He added: "Anyone who approaches this case as some kind of 'done deal' has got this very badly wrong. She loved her job, she cared deeply about the babies, and also cared for their families". She denies all 22 charges against her.

Mr Myers addressed each of the seven murder charges in turn and explained why Letby was not responsible. In the case of Child A, a twin boy, of which Letby is accused of injecting with air. He said that the defence did not accept that an air embolus or bubble, caused the child's death. He described the care of Child A who was born nine weeks prematurely in June 2015, as 'sub-optimal'. The second child allegedly killed by Letby, Child C, was described as 'very premature' having been born at 30 weeks, and weighing less than 2 lbs. Letby is accused of injecting him with air through a 'nasogastric tube'. Mr Myers stressed that such babies were particularly vulnerable to infection.

Child C should have received care at a specialist children's hospital. Child D, a full-term baby girl allegedly murdered by Letby by injecting air into her bloodstream, had also received poor care. Mr Myers said that it was 'beyond dispute' that the child should have been prescribed antibiotics hours before she was treated. There was also evidence that infection was a contributary factor in her death.

In the case of Child E, there was no satisfactory explanation for his death; a twin allegedly attacked in the presence of his mother. Letby is accused of injecting this child, who weighed just 3 lbs, with a fatal mount of air. However, Mr Myers remarked that "It is not right to rely on the assumption of guilt". He also stressed that that defence did not accept that Letby caused any harm to Child I. This was a girl born at just 27 weeks gestation, and who Letby allegedly attempted to kill on three separate occasions. She is accused of killing Child I on her fourth attempt. In relation to this victim, Mr Myers said: "We will say her collapses and death were part of a 'series of clinical problems' which may well have been inevitable given her extreme prematurity".

Mr Myers stated that there was no evidence that Letby harmed the final alleged victims, two of a set of triplets who died in June 2016. Letby is accused of carrying out her final attack on one of the triplets just 13 minutes after his brother died through her actions.

The first triplet was allegedly physically attacked. Child O had liver damage and had been injected with air into his bloodstream and stomach. This baby died towards the end of Letby's shift around 6 pm in June 2016. However, before she left the hospital for the night, Letby once again injected air into the nasogastric tube of the brother Child P, the prosecution claim. He died at 4 pm the following day, less than 24 hours after his brother. It appears that Letby later spent time with the boys' parents and even took a photograph of the dead infants together in their cot. The third triplet was not targeted and survived. Letby was removed from working on the unit. The court heard that the mother of a premature baby allegedly killed by Letby, found it difficult to accept the news that her son had stopped breathing without any warning.

The newborn Child C was according to doctors, 'doing all that was expected of him'. He was born weighing just 1 lb, 12 oz, and taken to the neonatal unit in the hospital. Days later, the mother who was on a post-natal ward, was woken up and instructed to go and see her son 'urgently'. Child C is one of the seven babies it is alleged Letby killed by injecting air into his stomach. The mother was told that his heart rate had suddenly dropped, and he had stopped breathing 'without any prior warning'.

The court heard in a statement from the mother's husband who said that Letby, whom he recognised from pictures in newspapers, was one of two nurses with them before the baby died. He said that one of the nurses, which could have been Letby, brought a ventilator basket in and said: "You've said your goodbyes, do you want me to put him in here?" He said that this insensitive comment from Letby, shocked them because their son was "not dead at that point".

The court heard that doctors at the hospital were 'baffled' by the increased mortality rate and could not find a 'medical cause'. Mr Johnson for the prosecution, said that babies who had not been unstable suddenly deteriorated for no apparent reason. Having searched for a logical reason which they were unable to find, the consultants noticed that the unexpected collapses and subsequent deaths did have one 'common denominator', the presence of Lucy Letby.

The court was told that police were called into the hospital and discovered that at least two boys from separate sets of twins had been deliberately poisoned with insulin eight months apart. These boys referred to as Child F and Child L, were two days old when they were allegedly attacked but survived. Mr Johnson, prosecuting, said the fact that Child F and Child L were deliberately injected with insulin will help the jury to interpret what happened to the other victims, and decide whether there was somebody 'sabotaging them' or whether they were just tragic coincidences.

Mr Johnson remarked that the collapses and deaths of the 17 children were not naturally occurring tragedies. He continued: "They were all the work of the woman in the dock... she... was the 'constant malevolent presence', when things took a turn for the worse for those 17 infants".

The jury was told that Child F was poisoned eight months later in April 2016. Mr Johnson said: "Lucy Letby was on duty when both of the children were poisoned, and we allege she was the poisoner". He told the court that Child F's brother, Child E, was murdered by Letby when she injected air into his bloodstream the day before she attacked his brother. He said that Child L's twin brother, Child M, was also attacked on the same day with air injected into his circulatory system, but he survived. The court heard that although doctors had realised Child F's and Child L's blood-sugar levels were dangerously low, they initially assumed it was a 'naturally occurring phenomenon'.

Mr Johnson said: "It simply did not occur to the medical staff that someone in the neonatal unit would have injected them with insulin. Nobody thought there was someone trying to kill babies". The jury were shown a chart of around 30 members of staff who worked in the unit, with an 'X' marking those who were present when each child was harmed. This graph displayed a long column of 'X's' below Letby's name, meaning she was present when all the babies collapsed or died. No other member of staff was present more than seven times.

Mr Johnson said Child A was born almost nine weeks early, but in good condition in June 2015. His notes recorded he was stable in the neonatal unit. However, at 8:26 pm the following day, soon after Letby began her night shift, he suffered a fatal collapse. Doctors noticed a 'pink rash over blue skin' which they had never seen before, which Mr Johnson said was a 'hallmark of the case' and a common occurrence in several other victims. A post-mortem failed to find a cause of death, but medical expert Dr Dewi Evans, later concluded that Child A died because 'air had been injected into his bloodstream'.

The jury heard that Letby was the only nurse to witness Child A's collapse. This occurred around the time she set up a glucose infusion. It is claimed the infusion would have given her access to a tube used to administer fluids into the baby's bloodstream. When interviewed by police more than three years later, Letby said that she had wondered whether the bag of fluid given to Child A was "not what we thought it was".

Mr Johnson pointed out that comment was 'an interesting turn of phrase' as experts have since concluded that the poisoner allegedly put insulin in the fluid bag of both Child F and Child L when they were attacked. Letby claimed that it was another nurse who had administered the glucose and that she had asked for the fluid to be examined after Child A's death. However, there was no record of Letby's request.

Mr Johnson added that the following day around

midnight, Child A's twin sister, Child B, also collapsed when Letby was on duty, soon after she had helped to set up a bag of intravenous feed with another nurse. Experts again concluded Child B's care had been 'sabotaged' by air being injected into her bloodstream.

Mr Johnson said that Letby told police officers Child B had similar 'rash' on her skin as that seen in her brother the previous day. She also admitted that it was her signature only on Child B's medical notes. However, NHS rules stipulate two nurses must sign when drugs are administered to a baby. The prosecution claimed Letby had overfed Child G with milk delivered through a nasogastric tube or had injected air into the tube.

It was further alleged that the nurse made two further attempts to kill Child G. The child survived but remains with quadriplegic cerebral palsy as the result of 'oxygen depravity'. Expert witness Dr Dewi Evans, a retired paediatrician, told the court that the 'only explanation for Child G's collapse was that she was 'force fed' a massive amount of milk and probably air. The baby had received far more than 45 ml of milk.

Prosecution expert neonatologist Dr Sandie Bohin, told the jury: "Babies do not take in air when vomiting. If they are vomiting, things are coming out, not going in".

Letby denied attempting to kill Child G on 7 September 2015. Dr Evans said that the excessive milk and air in Child G's stomach stopped her diaphragm working correctly, which restricted her breathing. Prolonged oxygen deprivation left the infant with brain damage. Letby allegedly tried to murder a premature baby girl within two hours of her birth.

The jury was told that Letby 'interfered' with the breathing tube of Child K. Consultant, Dr Ravi Jayaram, interrupted her. Child K had been born 15 weeks early at 25 weeks gestation, on 17 February 2016. Despite weighing only 1 lb, 8 oz, she was described as being in an 'expected and satisfactory' condition when she was delivered at 2:12 am. However, at 3:50 am, around an hour after she was admitted to the hospital neonatal unit, and when the nurse allocated to look after Child K left the room, she suddenly collapsed. Mr Johnson told the jury: "The allegation is Lucy Letby interfered with the endotracheal breathing tube and Dr Jayaram walked into the immediate aftermath".

However, Ben Myers KC, defending, told the court that the 'probable cause' for the tube dislodgement was that the child inadvertently moved it. Child K recovered after the tube was removed and was transferred to Arrowe Park Hospital on the Wirral but sadly died three days later.

The prosecution alleged that Letby attempted to murder Child K, but not that she caused her death. In a statement read to the court, the child's mother said the decision to turn off their daughter's life-support was the hardest of her life.

The parents of a newborn triplet begged doctors to take him to a different hospital after Letby allegedly murdered his two brothers with 24 hours, the court was told. Child O died on Letby's first shift on duty following a holiday break. The court heard that Letby was in 'floods of tears' after Child P, who was awaiting transfer to Liverpool Women's Hospital, died. After transport arrived, the parents begged them to take their surviving son.

In a distressing video interview with detectives, the triplet's father said: "We said there was no way he's staying at this hospital, you've got to take him". They agreed to take him and he spent several weeks before going home.

It transpired that management at the Chester hospital tried to get Letby back on duty against the wishes of doctors and refused to call in the police for 11 months, the court was told. Retired consultant paediatrician, John Gibbs, said he and his colleagues did not want the suspected killer nurse working on the neonatal unit after two triplets died suddenly under her care. He told the court that "even after she was eventually removed from work, managers resisted calls for police to be involved and tried to get her back on the ward. Doctors took the unusual step of 'demanding' CCTV be installed at the unit if Letby was to be allowed back", Dr Gibbs said.

In any event, the court heard that neither of these demands were met. Letby was finally arrested by police in July 2018 around two years after the two triplets died. In the 11 months before the police became involved, and following concerns raised about the triplets' deaths, senior managers were very reluctant to involve police to discuss what was taking place. Dr Gibbs was asked why he himself had not contacted the police. Dr Gibbs responded: "That was difficult. Nurse Letby seemed to be involved in all the cases that involved myself. Other consultants were involved with other babies. It is regrettable that none of us realised two babies had been poisoned with insulin, so we didn't have the full picture".

It was only after the two triplets, Child O and Child P, died, that Letby was finally taken off the ward in June 2016. Soon after Child P's death, Dr Stephen Brearey telephoned the hospital executive on duty, Karen Rees to demand Letby not be allowed to work the following day until an investigation was carried out. Mrs Rees refused and it is alleged that Letby tried to kill another premature baby boy the following day. Jurors were informed that Letby launched a formal grievance process after she was allocated to other duties away from the neonatal unit.

Letby began giving evidence at Manchester Crown Court on 2 May 2023, seven months into her trial. The prosecution say that she killed seven babies, five boys and two girls, and tried to murder another ten between June 2015 and June 2016. Letby is accused of injecting babies with air, poisoning them with insulin, overfeeding them with milk and physically assaulting them. Letby repeatedly denied trying to kill or murder 17 infants. Asked by her defence counsel, Ben Myers KC, whether she ever wanted to harm the babies, she replied: "I only ever did my best to care for them. I am there to help and care, not to hurt. It was sickening to be blamed for the deaths. I just couldn't believe it. It was devastating. I don't think you could be accused of anything worse than that".

Letby admitted describing doctors, including the consultant Ravi Jayaram who was in charge of the children's ward, and who pointed the finger at her, as 'bastards'. The court heard that he and other consultants blocked Letby from returning to the unit when she was moved into an office job in July 2016, despite the fact that hospital managers wanted her back on the ward. Asked if she ever wanted to hurt any of the many babies she looked after, Letby replied: "No, that's completely against everything a nurse is".

Mr Myers asked Letby to explain a note that police found at her home when she was arrested, two years after her final alleged victim died. Letby had written number of chaotic phrases including: "I don't deserve to live", "I killed them on purpose because I'm not good enough. I am a horrible evil person", and "I AM EVIL I DID THIS".

Letby claimed she wrote the note in July 2016 when she was "really struggling and doubting her professional ability".

Mr Myers asked: "How were you feeling?". She replied: "I felt immense responsibility. I felt I had been incompetent or done something wrong that had harmed the children". He pointed to a section of the brief note on which she had written: "I will never have children, or marry or know what it's like to have a family". Asked why, she replied: "because at that time I didn't see any future for myself. I couldn't imagine what life would be or that I would have a future". Mr Myers added: "The note says "I killed them on purpose because I'm not good enough". Why did you think you weren't good enough?"

Letby answered: "Because the suggestion throughout was that I'd done some wrong, that my competence had to be rechecked". Mr Myers asked her about the times she thought about killing herself and about the comment: "I'm evil, I did this". She told the jury: "I felt at that time if I'd done something wrong and I didn't know I'd done something, I must be such an awful evil person if I'd made mistakes and not known".

Letby said she started working at the Chester hospital while studying for her nursing degree at the city's university in 2010. She qualified the following September. Mr Myers also questioned her about a close relationship she had with a doctor. Asked whether there was 'anything more to the relationship', Letby replied: "No, he was just a trusted friend". But she admitted they had met up outside work, adding: "Sometimes we would go out for meals or coffee or walks". She said that friendship 'fizzled out' at the beginning of 2018 before she was arrested in July.

"Doctors conspired to blame Lucy Letby for the deaths and collapses of premature babies, to cover up for failings at their hospital". Letby claimed that four consultants at the hospital were part of a 'gang' who was out to 'get her'. She told the court that Dr Stephen Brearey who was in charge of the neonatal unit, Dr Ravi Jayaram, the lead consultant on the children's ward, Dr John Gibbs, and another female were trying to pin the deaths onto her. She said she was not responsible for attacking any baby. She also denied getting a thrill from photographing a sympathy card she sent to the parents of a baby girl she allegedly killed.

Cross-examined for a second day, Nick Johnson KC prosecuting, asked Letby: "Are you suggesting there's some sort of agreement between medical staff to get you?" Letby replied: "It's the consultant's group, I do believe, yes". Mr Johnson continued: "Four doctors. A gang of four let's call them. What's the conspiracy?". Letby replied:

"They have apportioned blame on to me". Mr Johnson said: "The motive?" Letby replied: "I believe to cover failings at the hospital". Earlier, Mr Johnson had suggested Letby was the 'only common feature' and had to be the person responsible for harming the babies from June 2015 to June 2016. The jury was shown a graph of shift patterns of every nurse on duty during the deaths and collapses. This showed Letby was the only one working each time.

Mr Johnson asked: "Do you agree that if certain combinations of those children were attacked then unless there was more than one person attacking them, you have to be the attacker?" Letby replied: "No. I have not attacked anyone. Just because I was on shift doesn't mean I have done anything".

Lucy Letby 'cooked' medical notes in a bid to cover her tracks, following the collapse of a baby in her care. The nurse allegedly faked the time a girl collapsed to link it to a milk feed given by a colleague.

She also deliberately altered the baby's temperature on her observation chart to make it appear as if she was poorly before she stopped breathing, it is claimed. Nick Johnson KC, prosecuting, questioned Letby about two allegations of attempted murder against the infant known as Child G.

Child G had been born weighing just over 1 lb at 23 weeks gestation in May 2015. Letby is charged with attacking her three times on two milestones in her life, on her 100th day, and a fortnight later. The child survived but suffered brain damage. Letby murdered two premature triplets less than 24 hours apart to get the attention of a doctor she had a 'crush' on, it was alleged at her trial. She denied 'sabotaging' and attacking the infants known as Child O and Child P, because she enjoyed being in a 'crisis situation', with the medic, who was described as her 'boyfriend'. Letby had previously said she 'loved' the doctor as a friend, but denied that she had a 'crush' or was 'sweet' on him. She insisted that their friendship was 'platonic'. Mr Johnson accused her of 'enjoying the drama of the babies' deaths'. "Did you enjoy being in these crisis situations with the doctor?" Mr Johnson asked. "No" replied Letby. "Did it give you something to talk about?" asked Mr Johnson. "No, he was a friend" she replied. Mr Johnson said that immediately after the second triplet died, Letby was texting another nurse, who was off duty and enjoying a day at the races to tell her what had happened. "Did you enjoy the drama?" Mr Johnson asked. "No, she was asking me", Letby replied.

Mr Johnson reminded the jury of text messages exchanged between Letby and her doctor friend on the morning of 23 June 2016, which was the day Child O died. In one message, she wrote 'boo' when he told her he was in a clinic until late morning. Mr Johnson asked: "Were you disappointed he wasn't there?" She replied: "Yes, I enjoyed working with him". Mr Johnson added: "Did you want to get his attention?". "No" replied Letby.

It is the prosecution case that Letby, who was the nurse in charge of Child O, overfed him milk around 12:30 pm and sabotaged his care again at 3:00 pm by injecting air into his stomach. On both occasions, she called her doctor friend to review Child O, but denied doing so to get his 'personal attention'. The doctor left the unit but was called back a third time just over an hour later when Child O collapsed for a final time.

Mr Johnson reminded Letby of the evidence of Dr Stephen Brearey, the head of the neonatal unit, and the triplet's parents who all described seeing an 'unusual' moving rash in Child O's swollen stomach as medics battled unsuccessfully to save his life. It is alleged that Letby caused this rash and Child O's fatal collapse by injecting air into his circulation, thereby blocking the flow of blood to his heart. Child O was pronounced dead at 5:47 pm and Mr Johnson said that within minutes Letby was sabotaging his brother Child P's care by 'pumping air' into his stomach via his nasal feeding tube, before she clocked off for the day. The third triplet survived and is not involved in the case. Child P collapsed three times on the following day shift while Letby was looking after him. She is accused of injecting him with air again and dislodging his breathing tube.

Mr Johnson reminded her of the evidence of another doctor who recalled Letby told her that Child P, who medics were attempting to transfer to a more specialised hospital, that he was "not leaving here alive". Letby said she couldn't recall making the comment and denied being 'excited' and behaving inappropriately immediately after the second triplet's death. The court heard that the triplets were extremely rare because they were identical, and had been conceived naturally, which happens in just one in 200 million births. Although seven weeks early, they weighed between 4 lbs and 5 lbs, and were born in good condition. Letby admitted that the triplets' arrival was 'big news' in the unit and that she had never seen naturally conceived triplets before. Ahead of her return to work, she texted a friend saying she would 'probably be back with a bang'.

Prosecution Closing Speech

Prosecuting Counsel Mr Nick Johnson KC, told the jury: "Lucy Letby is a cold-bloodied and calculating murderer who 'gas-lighted' her colleagues into believing the deaths of premature babies were a 'stroke of bad luck'. The 33-year-old neonatal nurse got away with harming infants because no-one was contemplating foul play". He added that she used methods of murdering and attempting to kill that "didn't leave much of a trace" and persuaded colleagues that the deaths were 'quite normal' when, in reality, she was 'cold, calculating, cruel and relentless'. Addressing the jury, at the start of his closing speech, Mr Johnson said: "We suggest that Lucy Letby gas-lighted staff at the hospital, doctors and nurses alike, professional people with many, many years of combined experience. She persuaded them that what they knew in their heart of hearts, to be utterly abnormal, was just a 'run of bad luck'.

Mr Johnson said Letby got away with her campaign of violence for so long because staff did not contemplate 'the remotest possibility of a nurse trying to kill tiny babies'. Letby targeted sick children and used the vulnerabilities of others, including a boy who had haemophilia, a blood disorder, to cover up her attacks. Mr Johnson said Letby also tried to cover her tracks by 'faking' nursing notes and asking colleagues to sign handwritten medical charts to deflect attention away from herself.

Nick Johnson told the eight women and four men of the jury: "Lucy Letby had used ways of killing that didn't leave much of a trace, certainly nothing was spotted at the time as being significant. Her behaviour persuaded many colleagues that the collapses and deaths were 'quite normal'. Many of them simply couldn't see the 'wood for the trees'. Several post-mortem examinations in isolation didn't raise alarm because no one was contemplating the possibility of foul play."

Mr Johnson said there were similarities between what happened to the 17 alleged victims that proved Letby was the 'single person 'sabotaging children.

Blood tests unearthed by police years after the children fell ill and died, now 'proved' that two of the babies known as Child F and Child L, were poisoned by insulin. Letby admitted the boys, who were from separate sets of twins, born seven months apart, 'had been poisoned but she was not at fault'. In Child F's case, Letby was so 'sly' she even poisoned a stock bag of intravenous feed which she knew would be used in his drip when she was off duty. Child F was the only baby receiving feed on the unit at the time.

"What better way for a poisoner to cover their tracks than to leave a replacement bag in the fridge to be used by an unsuspecting colleague?" Mr Johnson said. "This shows a degree of cynical, cold-bloodied planning. It diverts suspicion on to someone else and deflects suspicion from Lucy Letby".

Letby targeted Child F because she had murdered his twin brother Child E, by injecting air into his bloodstream the day before, on 4 August 2015. Mr Johnson said Child L had double the amount of insulin in his blood as did Child F. This speaks volumes. It is alleged Letby added a drug to Child L's drip of dextrose on at least two occasions. She also tried to murder his twin brother, Child M, by injecting him with air on the same shift in April 2016. Both babies fortunately survived.

Mr Johnson told the jury that the person who poisoned Child F must have poisoned Child L. "The idea that two people on this neonatal unit were separately 'spiking' fluid bags is so improbable that it can be discarded. Child F survived, so the poisoner, Lucy Letby, upped the dose for Child L. What clearer evidence than an intention to kill could you have?"

Mr Johnson told the jury that if they concluded Letby murdered Child E and tried to murder Child F, Child L and Child M, then it put 'all the other cases into a very clear context'.

Letby claimed a 'gang of four' consultants conspired to blame her for the collapses and deaths to cover up for failings in the babies' care. Mr Johnson concluded: "Not only is Lucy Letby prepared to kill babies, she is also prepared to blatantly trash" the reputations of responsible professional people. He asked the jury: "Do you really think they would say things they knew were not true to get Lucy Letby convicted?"

Defence Closing Speech

"The case against Lucy Letby is 'fuelled by the presumption of guilt'. The prosecution has 'twisted' and changed their theory to fit claims that the neonatal nurse killed and harmed babies in her care" Letby's counsel told the court. Mr Ben Myers KC said that whatever Letby did could be considered an affirmation of her 'guilt'. He added: "What really is at work is best described as a presumption of guilt, and this prosecution case is fuelled by it and riddled by it. No matter what Lucy Letby says, does or doesn't do is slotted into the ever-flexible, ever-changing theory of guilt, everything is treated as 'evidence of guilt". Mr Myers concluded by identifying two possibilities for the spike in baby collapses and deaths at the Chester hospital from June 2015 to June 2016.

"The first was that they were due to medical conditions of the babies as well as the staffing pressures and failings in care. The other was that a 'dedicated' neonatal nurse had decided to kill children or try to kill them for reasons beyond comprehension."

On 10 July 2023, after a nine-month trial, the jury was sent out to deliberate. It was not until 8 August that verdicts were returned after a period of several days. However, it was not until the final verdicts were returned on 18 August 2023, that they were made public.

Letby was found guilty of seven counts of murder of seven babies. She was also found guilty of seven counts of attempted murder of six babies. She was found not guilty of two counts of attempted murder.

The jury was unable to reach verdicts on six further attempted murder charges. On 21 August, 2023, Letby was sentenced to 'life imprisonment' with a whole life order, the most severe sentence possible in English law.

After the trial, Lucy Letby was remanded to HMP Prison Low Newton, a closed women's facility in County Durham.

"On Monday, 21 August 2023, Lucy Letby received 14 whole-life prison terms. She delivered a 'final act of wickedness' to victims by refusing to appear in the court dock to hear her fate, staying in the cells below the court. After being found guilty of murdering seven babies, and attempting to murder six more, after a ten-month trial, those whose lives she destroyed described her as 'evil disguised as a caring nurse' who treated each infant as 'just a pawn in her sick, twisted game' and 'collateral damage', The trial judge, Mr Justice Goss, insisted on Letby being handed his sentencing remarks and copies of the harrowing victim impact statements, written by the families of those she preyed on. Britain's worst serial child murderer of modern criminal history, becomes only the fourth woman sentenced to die behind bars".

Source: Daily Mail, 22, August, 2023. Authors: Richard Marsden and Lucy Hull.

Transcript of Mr Justice Goss's Sentencing Remarks

The defendant, Lucy Letby, has refused to attend court for this sentence hearing. Accordingly, I have to sentence her in her absence. I shall deliver the sentencing remarks as if she was present to hear them and I direct that she is provided with a transcript of my remarks and copies of the Victim Personal Statements read to the court.

Lucy Letby, over a period of almost 13 months between June 2015 and June 2016, when in your mid-20s and employed as a neo-natal nurse at the Countess of Chester Hospital in Chester with specialist training in intensive care, you murdered seven babies and attempted to murder six others, in the case of one of them trying on separate occasions two weeks apart to murder her. You are now to be sentenced for your crimes. I order payment of the statutory surcharge in the appropriate amount.

You acted in a way that was completely contrary to the normal human instincts of nurturing and caring for babies and in gross breach of the trust that all citizens place in those who work in the medical and caring professions. The babies you harmed were born prematurely and some were at risk of not surviving, but in each case, you deliberately harmed them, intending to kill them. In your evidence you said that 'hurting a baby is completely against everything that being a nurse is', as, indeed, it should be. You also claimed you never did anything that was meant to hurt a baby and only ever did your best to care for them. That was but one of the many lies you were found to have told in this case.

There is no doubt that you are intelligent and, outwardly, were a very conscientious hard working, knowledgeable, confident and professional nurse, which enabled you repeatedly to harm babies on the unit without arousing suspicion for some time. You prided yourself in your competence. Your fellow neonatal nurses spoke very highly of you, and several of them became your close friends. Having started as a Band 5 nurse at the Countess of Chester in 2012, you became a mentor to student nurses and, in the spring of 2015, gained the qualification that enabled you to care for the sickest babies on the unit or those requiring the most intensive care. You relished being in the intensive care nursery. Your messages to colleagues revealed an interest in babies that were on or were coming to the unit who had uncommon medical conditions.

The methods you employed to carry out your murderous intent were only revealed by the later detailed investigation into the events of and surrounding the collapses and deaths of the babies which commenced in 2018. There was premeditation, calculation and cunning in your actions. You specifically targeted twins and, latterly, triplets. Some babies were healthy, others had medical issues of which you were aware. The great majority of your victims suffered acute pain as a result of what you did to them. They all fought for survival; some, sadly, struggled in vain and died. You used a number of different ways to try to kill them, thereby misleading clinicians into believing the collapses had, or might have had a natural cause or were a consequence of developing medical condition. You took opportunities to harm babies when staff were on breaks or away from babies. On some occasions you falsified records to indicate there were signs of a deterioration before a collapse occurred. You knew that the last thing anyone working in the unit would or did think was that someone caring for the babies was deliberately harming them.

As the number of unexpected and unexplained collapses and deaths escalated, senior doctors started to 'think the unthinkable' and considerate possibility that someone was, in fact, deliberately harming the babies, and you were identified as the common factor. You had a detached enthusiasm for the resuscitations and what followed. You endeavoured to impress colleagues and clinicians and sought reassurance from them as to your competence and skills, and would message others to the effect that no-one was at fault. On occasions, your cruelty and callousness were revealed by making inappropriate remarks to some of the grieving parents at the time or in the immediate aftermath of a death. When the homes of both you and your parents were searched, confidential documents relating to babies, including handover and resuscitation sheets and notes and blood gas readings were found, and there were entries in a diary recording relevant events. Handover sheets relating to all but the first four of the babies had been taken from the unit and kept by you. I am satisfied you started to keep these documents after those initial offences in June 2015 as morbid records of the dreadful events surrounding the collapses of your victims and what you had done to them. You had a fascination with the babies and their families which extended to making repeated searches on Facebook for their parents, sometimes immediately following the events and, on occasions much later. A piece of paper with dense writing on both sides, setting out your thoughts and feelings, was found in the first search of your home in 2018. Amongst the phrases you wrote were 'the world is better off without me' and 'I am evil I did this'.

The impact of your crimes has been immense, as disclosed by the deeply moving personal statements that have been read to the court this morning. The lives of new-born or relatively new-born babies were ended almost as soon as they began and lifelong harm has been caused, all in horrific circumstances. Loving parents have been robbed of their cherished children and others have to live with the physical and mental consequences of your actions. Siblings have been deprived of brothers and sisters. You have caused deep psychological trauma, brought enduring grief and feelings of guilt, caused strains in relationships and disruption to the lives of all the families of all your victims.

It is no part of my function to reach conclusions as to the underlying reason or reasons for your actions. Nor could I, for they are known only to you. I must pass appropriate sentences according to law, addressing the seriousness of your offences, the facts of which I now describe briefly.

On the evening of 8th June 2015 you murdered 'A'. He died just over 24 hours after he was born, suddenly and unexpectedly collapsing shortly after you took over as his designated nurse at the start of the evening shift. He was in a nursery with is twin sister 'R'. Although he was born prematurely, he had been extremely stable. He died of air embolus as a result of you administering a bolus of air into his venous system which blocked off the blood supply to his heart and lungs. In common with all nurses, you knew from your training the dangers caused by air getting into the venous system and that air embolus was very rarely encountered in clinical practice. You took part in the attempts to resuscitate 'A' and claimed you found the process of taking his footprints and handprints, as well as photographs of him after his death, to be quite a nice thing to do for the baby and you saw it as a way of giving parents memories. In evidence, you sought to blame others for his collapse. The following day you searched for 'A's mother on Facebook and then, on the ensuing night shift, at shortly after midnight on 10th June, you attempted to murder his sister 'B', by injecting air into her venous system via a long line through which she was receiving nutrition. Fortunately, she was able to be resuscitated and survived.

Four days after 'B's' collapse, in the early hours of 14th June, 'C' collapsed and died in the intensive care nursery. He had been born four days earlier at 30 weeks gestation in good condition, but was vulnerable; he had a lung infection which was being treated by antibiotics. However, his breathing stabilised. He was being fed by a nasogastric tube. You messaged a colleague saying you 'needed to throw yourself back in and take an ITU baby soon'.

On that night shift of 13-14th June you were the designated nurse for two babies in another nursery. 'C' was started on trophic, that is tiny, feeds that night. You were at the side of his incubator when he stopped breathing and his oxygen saturations were very low as a result of you having deliberately infused an excessive amount of air down his nasogastric tube. Attempts to resuscitate 'C' failed and he died some hours later in his parents' arms. Before he passed away you made an insensitive and inappropriate but revealing comment to them about them having said their goodbyes and to put him in a ventilated basket. Understandably they reacted to this.

Just over a week later, in the early hours of Monday 22nd June, 'D' who had been born 36 hours earlier, died in the intensive care nursery. You will have been aware that she was being treated for an infection and were the designated nurse for 2 other babies in that nursery on that night shift. You decided to kill her and administered air into her intravenously, causing her to die from air embolus. You were involved in her resuscitation and, in your messaging with other nurses after 'D's death, you described how upsetting it was and how distraught her parents were and referred to thinking an element of fate was involved.

Three days after 'D' died, you searched for her parents on Facebook and, over three months later, on 3rd October you made two more searches for her father.

Over a month passed before you killed another baby. Again, it was a twin who was selected: 'E'. He and his brother 'F' were born on 29th July. 'E' died in the early hours of 4th August. During the shift that night you were the designated nurse for both 'E' and 'F'. 'E' died of air embolus and there was damage to his upper gastro-intestinal tract caused by trauma of some kind inflicted by you, which resulted in significant blood loss. The bleeding started earlier in the shift and was seen by his mother; she was very concerned and you sought to reassure her. The circumstances of the attempted resuscitation and his death were harrowing, with profuse bleeding. At the time the clinicians thought he may have died of necrotising enterocolitis and no post mortem was undertaken. You commented in messages to colleagues that he had a massive haemorrhage and it could have happened to anyone.

On the following nightshift, the 4th-5th August, you turned your attention to 'F' and poisoned him by adding manufactured insulin to his intravenous infusion of total parenteral feed. Only very small volumes of insulin needed to be added to the half-litre bags of feed; it was not noticeable in the bag, nor would it be apparent that any was missing from the insulin bottle. You infused a bag that was hung that shift and several other stock bags.

As a result, when bags were changed, 'F' continued to have dangerously low blood sugar levels despite increasing infusions of dextrose. It was only when a bag that had not had insulin added was hung that his levels recovered and he was no longer at risk of the consequences of hypoglycaemia of brain damage and potential death. 'F' recovered but has severe learning difficulties. No doubt you were assured that no-one suspected that insulin had been added and, with this knowledge, you went on to repeat this method of attempting to kill another twin 'T', some eight months later. Again, you made Facebook searches. On 6th August and 14th September, you searched for his mother and you searched for both parents in October.

In September you made two attempts to kill 'G'. She was a very premature baby who was born in Arrowe Park Hospital on 31st May at only 23 weeks and six days' gestation. Although on the margin of survival, she did survive. By 13th August she was stable and was transferred to the Countess of Chester, where the general trend of improvement continued. The 7th September was her 100th day of life; nurses had planned a small celebration, including the display of a banner. On the nightshift of 6th-7th, you deliberately injected milk and air into 'G's stomach down the nasogastric tube shortly after her designated nurse had fed her, causing her to projectile vomit; her alarms sounded, her heart rate and saturation levels dropped and she required breathing assistance. You were nearby and assisted, and later sought to blame a colleague for potentially over-feeding. In messaging prior to 'G' being transferred back to Arrowe Park in the early hours of 8th September, you referred to her being a 'high risk baby'. Five days after 'G's return to the Countess of Chester on 16th September, you made a further attempt to kill her on 21st September by over-feeding her, causing her to projectile vomit again and stop breathing and her saturations dropped. 'G' suffered a severe and profound injury to her brain from the first event on 7th September, which may have been added to by your actions on 21st September, and from which she will not recover. She requires constant nursing care and attention and will require surgery and support throughout her life.

Just over a month later, on 23rd October, you murdered 'H'. She had been born at Arrowe Park Hospital on 7th August and had been at the Countess of Chester from 18th

August, apart from two short periods in September and October. When at the Countess of Chester, she suffered a series of sudden, unexpected and unexplained episodes. On 30th September you infused a large quantity of air down her nasogastric tube into her stomach and bowel, thereby interfering with her breathing, reducing her oxygen saturations and heart rate and causing her to vomit and require oxygen under pressure.

It is also likely that, in the early hours of 13th October, you infused air into her venous system. The following night she collapsed again but recovered with breathing support and was transferred to Arrowe Park for two days. Six days after her return, on the night of 22nd-23rd October, she suffered her final collapse, crying out in severe pain as a result of air embolus after you had injected air into her venous system. She too, died in her parents' arms. Not only was it devastating for 'H's family, it was also deeply upsetting for the nursing and medical staff, who had known and cared for 'H' for some time and had fought to save her. Again, you searched for her mother on Facebook.

In early April 2016, you administered insulin to 'T' and injected air into the venous system of his twin brother, 'J', repeating what you had done eight months earlier to twins 'E' and 'F'. They had been born on 8th April. You added insulin to the dextrose bag that was set up for 'I' within two hours of his birth and to several other bags that were later hung. On 9th April, when 'I' was hypoglycaemic, you injected air into 'J's venous system causing him to suffer a profound apnoeic episode and cardio-respiratory arrest. It took just under 30 minutes to resuscitate him. You were present throughout. A piece of paper towel on which details of the drug administration notes had been noted during the emergency and a blood gas print out which you had retrieved from the confidential waste were found at your home after your arrest, and you also took home handover sheets relating to 'J'. You made a note of the event in your diary. J suffered irreversible brain damage as a result of his cardio-respiratory collapse and, over time, he may well deviate from his peers in relation to attainment and cognitive or motor function.

On the 3rd June you attempted to murder 'K'. He had been born on 2nd June. His mother is haemophiliac. This interested you. When his designated nurse went on a break in the early hours of the night after he was born, you inflicted some painful trauma in the pharynx area causing him to scream, bleed and profoundly desaturate. Fortunately, he survived but could have suffered the consequences of the trauma to his throat.

Almost a week later on 21st June 2016 'XY' gave birth to identical triplet boys. Although on holiday at the time, you were communicating with colleagues about the triplets and said you felt most at home in the intensive care nursery. On your first day back at work on 23rd June you were the designated nurse for 'L' and 'M' who, together with their brother 'O', were all in the intensive care nursery. That afternoon 'L' suffered a series of sudden and unexpected collapses as a result of you administering air down his nasogastric tube as well as into his venous system., and you inflicted trauma to his liver causing significant bleeding.

The horror of the consequences of your actions, and the desperate attempts to resuscitate him and save his life, sadly to no avail, were vividly described by clinicians and his father. The following day you murdered his older brother 'M'. You forced air down his nasogastric tube into his stomach and bowel, and inflicted trauma to his liver but not damaging it as severely as you had in 'L's case. The air caused his diaphragm to splint and he collapsed. His life could not be saved. His father remembered him struggling for his life like his brother. 'O' was removed to another hospital and to safety. In messages to a friend and colleague, when investigations into the unexpected collapses and deaths on consecutive days were under way, you referred to the risk of air embolus and you submitted a Datix report, which you did in a totally unrelated case on 1st July, referring to one of the lumens through which intravenous medication was being administered via an umbilical venous catheter being open. The cruelty and calculation of your actions were truly horrific.

After these last collapses and deaths, you were suspended from nursing duties but pursued complaints of being treated unfairly. When you home was later searched, as well as your 2016 diary, which contained references to long days on 23rd, 24th and 25th June and to 'L' and 'M', there were handover sheets over that period with resuscitation notes written on the back. All, I have no doubt, being records that you kept to remind you of the details of the consequences of what you had done to those children.

For the offence of murder, the sentence is fixed by law and is imprisonment for life. You are now 33 years of age and were 21 when you committed the offences. Pursuant to the relevant prevailing statutory regime, by having regard to Schedule 21 to the Criminal Justice Act 2003, I have to determine whether the seriousness of the offences of murder, individually or in combination, is so exceptionally high that I should not make a minimum term order and you should spend the rest of your life in prison. For offences of attempted murder, whole life sentences of imprisonment are reserved for wholly exceptional cases. Over a period of just under 13 months you killed seven fragile babies and attempted to kill six others. Some of your victims were only a day or a few days old. All were extremely vulnerable. They were in a hospital where others were striving to provide them with dedicated medical and nursing care. By their nature and number, such murders and attempted murders by a neo-natal nurse entrusted to care for them are offences of very exceptional seriousness. The damaging impact of your actions on others working at that hospital, including those who numbered you as a friend, betraying their trust and creating upset and suspicion, as well as eroding confidence in clinicians and nurses generally, aggravates their seriousness.

This was a cruel, calculated and cynical campaign of child murder involving the smallest and most vulnerable children, knowing that your actions were causing significant physical suffering and would cause untold mental suffering. You created situations so that collapses or causes of collapses would not be obvious or associated with you; you removed and retained confidential records of events relating to your crimes and checked up on bereaved parents. There was a deep malevolence bordering on sadism in your actions. During the course of this trial, you have coldly denied any responsibility for your wrongdoing and sought to attribute some fault to others. You have shown no remorse. There are no mitigating factors. In their totality, the offences of murder and attempted murder were of exceptionally high seriousness and just punishment, according to law, requires a whole life order.

Lucy Letby, on each of the seven offences of murder and the seven offences of attempted murder, I sentence you to imprisonment for life. Because the seriousness of your offences is exceptionally high, I direct that the early release provisions do not apply. The order of the court, therefore, is a whole life order on each and every offence and you will spend the rest of your life in prison.

Source: "Life Sentencing Remarks" (PDF), judiciary.gov.uk Manchester Crown Court, 21 August 2023.

The Lucy Letby Case Time Line

January 2012	Letby starts work at the Countess of Chester Hospital
8 June 2015	Letby murders Child A
9 June 2015	Letby attempts to murder Child B
14 June 2015	Letby murders Child C
22 June 2015	Letby murders Child D
June 2015	Internal review into the deaths
3 August 2015	Letby murders Child E
5 August 2015	Letby murders Child F
7 September 2015	Letby attempts to murder Child G
21 September 2015	Letby makes second attempt to murder Child G
30 September 2015	Letby attempts to murder Child I
12 October 2015	Letby makes second attempt to murder Child I
23 October 2015	Letby succeeds in murdering Child I
October 2015	Consultants meet with senior hospital management
February 2016	External reviews ordered
23/24 June 2016	Letby attempts to murder Child L and Child M
23 June 2016	Letby attempts to murder Child N and murders Child O
24 June 2016	Letby murders Child P
July 2016	Letby removed from working in the neonatal unit. Transferred to clerical duties in the hospital
September 2016	Letby commences grievance procedure about her removal from nursing duties
May 2017	Cheshire Police commence a criminal investigation
3 July 2018	Letby arrested

6 July 2018	Letby bailed
10 June 2019	Letby arrested for second time
13 June 2019	Letby bailed
10 November 2020	Letby arrested for third time
11 November 2020	Letby charged with 8 counts of murder and 10 counts of attempted murder
	Bail refused
10 October 2022	Letby's trial opens at Manchester Crown Court
18 August 2023	Letby found guilty of 14 of the 22 charges
21 August 2023	Letby sentenced to life-imprisonment with whole-life order

CHAPTER FOUR
The Aftermath

Lucy Letby was a neonatal nurse at the Countess of Chester Hospital NHS Trust. She was arrested three times from July 2018 to November, 2020, but was bailed twice pending further enquiries. While several reports had been filed since 2015 of a suspicious increase in the number of baby deaths and non-fatal collapses in the hospital, they were ignored or dismissed by the senior management at the hospital. This highlights issues with 'whistleblowing' and patient safety in the NHS, mainly attributed to the power imbalance between staff and senior management.

More than 500 consultants were interviewed for the 'After Lucy Letby: Silence on the Wards' ITV documentary. 71% of these consultants said their careers would be harmed if they raised any patient safety concerns. Reasons for this included bullying accusations, the threat of unfavourable regulator (General Medical Council) referrals, and potentially losing their jobs. Dr Ravi Jayaram, a consultant paediatrician at the Countess of Chester Hospital NHS Trust, called for a shift in NHS culture to facilitate greater accountability of staff behaviour. For example, developing an environment based on patient input and revising the appraisal process of senior NHS managers.

In response to the Letby case, the Department of Health and Social Care has implemented an inquiry led by as senior judge, Dame Kate Thirlwall. Inquiries involve investigations into issues of public concern for accountability or improvement purposes. Legal principles and considerations are scrutinised, particularly lawful decision making, fairness and due process. The inquiry into the Letby case covers three areas; the experiences of all the affected parents, the conduct of hospital staff and managers, and NHS culture. Moreover, NHS England is considering the regulation of non-clinical NHS managers. This includes exploring recommendations posed in the Kark Review regarding banning senior managers in the case of misconduct. Dr Henrietta Hughes, the Patient Safety Commissioner for England, supports using an Accredited Register to conduct a regulatory check on senior managers. Reforms are needed to ensure consistent competency standards across trusts, considering the Care Quality Commission's inaccurate report in 2016 of 'good leadership and communication' in the Countess of Chester NHS Trust, despite senior management's dismissal of and delayed responses to staff concerns about Lucy Letby.

The Lucy Letby case exposed flaws in the UK's health care system regarding 'whistleblowing' and patient safety. In response, a statutory inquiry is being conducted and the UK government has prepared several measures to address these issues.

Source: Legal Advice Centre, 26, February, 2024. Author: Marion Mahor.

A consultant who tried to 'blow the whistle' on Lucy Letby, called for regulation of NHS executives to make them accountable for their decisions. Dr Stephen Brearey was one of seven senior medics who said he repeatedly tried to alert managers at the Chester hospital to the neonatal nurse's 'murder spree'. At least two babies died and more were harmed because executives refused to listen or to believe a member of staff was to blame. The parents whose new-born son was killed, and his twin poisoned by Letby, accused the hospital of a 'total fob-off' when they pleaded for answers. Dr Brearey said some form of regulatory body is needed akin to the General Medical Council who govern doctors, to scrutinise the activities of bosses, and stop the revolving door of NHS executives moving between hospital trusts.

"Doctors and nurses have regulatory bodies they have to answer to. Quite often senior managers who have no apparent accountability for what they do in NHS Trusts, move to other trusts. There does not seem to be any system of accountability, and for them to justify their actions in a 'systematic way".

His call has been backed by Sir Robert Francis KC, who led the inquiry into the Mid-Staffordshire NHS scandal. Dr Brearey said the "time has now come to set up a system where managers faced being 'struck off' for serious failings. Those found responsible for mismanagement and 'cock-ups' should also be 'blacklisted' to prevent them being appointed to new positions elsewhere within the NHS".

Tony Chambers, chief executive of the Countess of Chester Hospital, and the director of nursing, Alison Kelly, both moved on to lucrative positions elsewhere in the NHS after leaving the hospital. Dr Brearey sad consultants who complained or raised concerns to managers, were seen as a 'problem'. He said that, since Letby's conviction for seven murders and seven attempted murders, he had been contacted by other doctors at different hospitals, who had experienced similar treatment from managers, when they raised issues, but not of the same magnitude. "Sometimes clinicians raise concerns with senior managers of the hospital and their lives are made very difficult by doing that", Dr Brearey said. "I can't emphasise enough, what a difficult position that puts clinicians in. Not only do they feel the issue isn't being addressed, but they also feel under attack. Going to work every day and carrying out clinical practices in that environment is difficult". Dr Brearey suggested managers were motivated by a desire to protect their hospitals from reputational damage. "What was put out in our case, was fear of reputational damage for the organisation. I suspect underlying that is probably a fear of individual reputational damage as well", he said.

Solicitor Richard Scorer, of law firm Slater and Gordon, agreed regulation was a real concern within the NHS. "You can have scientifically trained clinicians raising concerns with managers in the NHS who do not necessarily have any scientific training. It is possible to be a manager in the NHS with a degree in sociology. It means there can be managers making life or death decisions without any accountability for those decisions", he said.
Source: Daily Mail, 23, August, 2023. Author: Liz Hull.

Lucy Letby was snared by a prosecution witness haunted by accounts of the screams of babies she killed. Dr Sandie Bohin was brought in by police in 2019 as officers investigated why so many premature babies had died on the neonatal ward where Letby worked. Sitting at her dining room table studying x-rays, the paediatrician refused to believe what she was seeing after spotting air bubbles, known as 'embolisms' in images of the babies' blood vessels. "I thought it can't be. I'd never seen anything like that in my career, but nothing else explained it. The x-rays were in front of me, several of them, all showing air in the babies' vessels. That's when I thought, "No, it has to be, and it has to be deliberate".

She was struck by accounts from parents and medics of the babies' 'screaming' before they collapsed and died. Harrowing accounts told how the defenceless children cried out for up to 30 minutes at a time, despite it being extremely rare for premature babies to 'scream at all'. Dr Bohin said the grim reality was that each baby was effectively suffering a heart attack, after Letby injected air into their bloodstream or stomach, causing lethal bubbles. The screams of agony could be heard outside the unit. She said: "I remember the mother of one of the babies said she could hear in the corridor her child making a noise that a baby should never be making. That will be forever etched on her memory".

Dr Bohin told the Sunday Times: "To have a premature baby screaming is really unusual. What was described on the ward was babies screaming for up to 30 minutes. This is just unheard of. Somebody had done something to cause those babies extreme pain. With an air embolus, the air can get locked into the heart and it can also get into one of the arteries which supplied oxygen to the heart muscle, and the baby effectively has a heart attack". A senior doctor at the neonatal unit warned that chaotic conditions meant it was unsafe for patients and staff, two years before Letby was suspended.

The paediatrician emailed the hospital Chief Executive Tony Chambers in late 2015, saying staff were in tears because they were 'chronically overworked' and forced to have more babies than could be safely cared for in the unit. The senior doctor (who cannot be named for legal reasons) wrote: "This is now our normal working position and it is not safe. Things are stretched thinner and thinner and are at breaking point". At the time of the email, also reported by the *Sunday Times*, the ward had a fifth fewer nurses than it should have had. Letby's trial heard that she volunteered for extra shifts and was often left alone with babies. The email was sent after she had murdered five and tried to kill three. She was eventually moved off the unit in 2016.

Source: Daily Mail, 28, August, 2023. Author: Vanessa Allen.

The public inquiry into Lucy Letby's crimes must be widened to examine the NHS's 'cover-up culture' and other failures in patient safety, the Health Service Ombudsman, Rob Behrens, has said. The inquiry should also look into why so many hospital bosses ignore concerns about lapses in safety, and victimise 'whistleblowers' who raise them. He wants the inquiry to investigate how the NHS generally deals with failings in care, as well as exploring how Letby was able to murder seven babies and try to kill six others, despite senior doctors raising the alarm about her. While the inquiry's first duty is to give the families of Lucy Letby's victims the answers they want, it should also explore how other hospitals have demonstrated the same 'cover-up' culture and dismissive attitude, that consultant paediatricians experienced at the Chester hospital.

Behrens said: "We need the inquiry to thoroughly examine the NHS leadership, accountability and culture to contextualise what happened. Among the many questions the inquiry will need to answer and without prejudice, is why did the leaders of this trust act in the way they did? And related to that, why do leaders in the wider NHS too often act in a way that prioritises protecting the 'reputation' of their organisation over patient safety? It should also look into why a raft of initiatives in recent years, which were intended to make it easier for staff to raise concerns and to force trusts to be more open about mistakes, have in their view, failed to achieve their aims? The 'whistleblowing law', the duty of candour and the accountability of NHS trust boards and executives are not working effectively. In 2014, NHS care providers in England were put under a new legal duty of candour. It obliged them to be 'open and transparent' with patients about lapses in patient safety, and to provide 'truthful information and an apology' when things go wrong. It is unacceptable that trusts still fail in meeting this duty, nearly a decade after it was introduced. The NHS still has a big problem when it comes to being open about patient safety", added Behrens.

Ministers initially said the Letby Inquiry would be non-statutory, which prompted widespread concern that it would not be able to compel witnesses to appear, or order the disclosure of documents. Following sustained criticism, Steve Barclay, the Health Secretary, announced last month, that there would be a 'full statutory public inquiry'. Families of Letby's victims welcomed the decision. Lady Justice Thirlwall, an appeal court judge, was appointed earlier this month as the head of the inquiry. She is now working with the families to set its terms of reference.

Paul Whiteing, Chief Executive of the patient safety charity, Action Against Medical Accidents (AAMA), also urged Barclay to broaden the inquiry's scope to make it NHS-wide. Whiteing said: "We need to acknowledge that the issues that have emerged in this case, such as the apparent delays in investigating the adverse trend in the unexplained deaths of babies, and clinical staff calling out concerns, only to be ignored and made to apologise, are not unique to this trust. It is NHS wide".

NHS leaders and ministers should "make the difficult decisions to take a 'wide-angle lens approach' to this case, and use the sadness of this tragedy to make a step-change to the culture and values of the NHS, and to ensure openness and transparency, are really embedded at every level from ward to board".

Whiteing wants Lady Justice Thirlwall to look in particular at how effective NHS trust boards are at exercising scrutiny and control over the hospitals' executives, and who 'whistleblowers' share their concerns with. The inquiry should also investigate whether arrangements governing Freedom to Speak Up Guardians, are robust and independent enough. These guardians are supposedly independent senior figures within trusts, often doctors, to whom staff can bring their concerns. Professor Philip Bonfield, the leader of the British Medical Association said: "We receive almost daily feedback that doctors' concerns are still being ignored and not acted upon because the 'endemic culture' within the NHS is not to know what could possibly be wrong. This culture of 'denial' seen at the highest level, has to stop".

Source: The Guardian, 15, September, 2023. Author: Denis Campbell, Health Policy Editor.

Lucy Letby may have killed three more babies and tried to murder another 15, it was claimed at her trial. Dr Dewi Evans, who gave expert evidence against the neo-natal nurse, raised fresh concerns about the deaths of children who were not part of the prosecution's case. He also had suspicions over the cases of five children who survived. All of these were likely to have had their 'breathing tubes' tampered with by Letby whose 'modus operandi' changed over time. Her legal team applied for permission to appeal against the convictions.

Dr Evans said: "Initially, I looked at 32 cases, and there are seven of those (not part of the trial) that require more scrutiny. These babies had illnesses that were life-threatening and three of them died. We need to look at them to see if they were placed in harm's way as well. They were poorly so it may be impossible to show 'beyond reasonable doubt' whether they were the victim of 'inflicted harm'. There are seven cases that concern me, which we need to look at more thoroughly. I will be contacting Cheshire Police to bring these cases to their attention".

Dr Evans said that following Letby's arrest in July 2018, he was asked to review the notes of another 48 babies not included in the trial, and found concerns with as many as 18. They go back to 2012, although most date back to June, 2014, 12 months prior to the first fatality. He said: "I found several cases that are 'highly suspicious', where an endotracheal tube, placed in a baby's throat when they need breathing support, had been displaced and had come out. These tubes can come out 'accidentally' but for so many to come out is very unusual, especially in what I consider to be a good unit. I suspect these tubes were displaced intentionally. Of the 18, there could be up to ten babies who were placed 'in harm's way'. As far as I know, they survived without suffering any long-term harm".

Dr Evans was the prosecution's main expert and gave evidence on 17 separate occasions over the ten-month trial. He added: "One thing we can be reasonably sure of is that Lucy Letby did not turn up to work one day and decide to inject a baby with air into their bloodstream. I think the 'modus operandi' evolved over time, tube displacement was probably something that she did". All of these babies reviewed by Dr Evans were born at the Countess of Chester Hospital, although he said he had heard 'anecdotally' concerns about babies with displaced breathing tubes at Liverpool Women's Hospital, cases that the police were looking into. Letby did her nursing training placements there in 2012 and 2015. Dr Evans said he was also suspicious that at least one other baby whose notes detailed that he had a high insulin level, may have been poisoned by Letby, around November, 2015. This occurred during the middle of the other two insulin cases; Child F, who was poisoned in August, 2015, and Child I, who had insulin deliberately 'administered' in his drip in April, 2016.

Dr Evans described the failure of doctors on the unit to appreciate the significance of blood- test results from Child F, as an 'awful tragedy'. "If they had acted on that, it would have stopped all the other deaths and collapses" he said.

Three more babies died and another four were harmed by Letby over the following ten months before she was eventually removed from the ward in June, 2016. Cheshire Police are reviewing notes of 4,000 babies admitted to the neo-natal units of both the Countess of Chester Hospital and Liverpool Women's Hospital, during the 'footprint' of Letby's five-year nursing career.

Their investigation, code named 'Operation Hummingbird' is ongoing, and they have not ruled out Letby being charged with more crimes. Following the trial, sources told *The Guardian* that detectives had identified around 30 other babies, in addition to the 17 who featured in the trial, who may have been harmed by Letby. All of these survived. Dr Evans urged detectives to look closely at the medical notes of the babies named on 257 nursing hand-over sheets discovered in Letby's house following her arrest. These sheets should have been destroyed in

'confidential waste' at the hospital at the end of each shift.
Source: Daily Mail, 18, September, 2023. Author: Liz Hull.

    Lucy Letby will face a retrial over an alleged attempted murder of a baby girl, a court was told. However, a lawyer acting for families of other alleged victims of the former neonatal nurse, said she was 'disappointed' that Letby would not face new prosecutions on all the charges the jury in her previous trial failed to reach verdicts on. Parents have been left with 'unanswered questions' the lawyer said, 'and they deserve to know what happened to their children'. In August, 2023, Letby was found guilty of the murder of seven premature babies, and the attempted murder of six others. She was cleared of a further two attempted murder charges. The jury failed to reach a decision on another six charges relating to five babies. On 25 September 2023, Letby listened via video-link from New Hall prison, West Yorkshire, as prosecutor Nick Johnson KC, told Manchester Crown Court that a decision had been made to pursue a retrial in the case of one of the infants, Child K, a girl born in February, 2016.
    Mr Johnson said the crown would not be pursuing retrial over the five other charges of attempted murder, relating to two girls, Child H and Child J, and two boys Child N and Child Q. Jonathan Storer, Chief Crown Prosecutor at Mersey-Cheshire Crown Prosecution Service, said lawyers had consulted with the families of the babies involved before deciding on which charges to pursue. Other factors, including the evidence heard during the trial, and its impact 'on our legal test for proceeding with a prosecution' had been considered. He added: "These decisions on whether to seek retrials on the remaining counts of attempted murder, 'were extremely complex and difficult", Mr Storer said.
    Letby, who was sentenced to 14 whole-life terms on 21 August 2023, has applied for leave to appeal against her conviction. Judge Mr Justice Goss, said the first available

date for the retrial, at the same court, which could last up to three weeks, was 10 June 2024.
Source: Daily Mail, 26, September, 2023. Author: Liz Hull.

The Royal Statistical Society (RSS) is calling for the Lucy Letby Inquiry to cover statistical evidence used in the trial, saying it can be difficult 'to draw conclusions from suspicious clusters of deaths' in hospitals. After the trial, a public inquiry was announced in a bid to unpick the circumstances around the crimes, and provide answers for the victims' families. It was later announced that the inquiry would become 'statutory', meaning it has the legal powers to compel witnesses to give evidence. Now experts have argued that the inquiry should not only cover medical evidence but 'statistical evidence' also.

In a letter to Lady Justice Thirlwall, who is leading the public inquiry, Dr Andrew Garrett, the President of the RSS, and Sarah Cumbers, its Chief Executive, stresses the importance of evidence based on statistics and data, and suggest a better understanding of the area could help NHS Trusts act more quickly in similar cases. However, the letter also notes there are potential pitfalls to avoid.

"It is far from straightforward to draw conclusions from 'suspicious clusters of deaths' in a hospital setting. It is a statistical challenge to distinguish 'event clusters' that arise from criminal acts from those that arise 'coincidentally' from other factors even if the data in question was collected with rigour", the authors said.

The RSS sent its 2022 report: 'Healthcare Serial Killer or Coincidence?' to both the prosecution and defence at the start of Letby's trial. It sets out statistical issues in the investigation of suspected medical misconduct. The letter by Garrett and Cumbers, however, suggests the judicial system could benefit from more guidance on the matter, calling for the inquiry to consider including a point in terms of reference, on the appropriate use of statistical evidence in this type of case.

Statistical evidence is one type of evidence that NHS Trusts might use to identify criminal activity, and it is important that the right lessons are learned, and that it is used appropriately. Professor David Spielgelhalter of the University of Cambridge, welcomed the letter from the RSS. "Finding whether something is too surprising to be just a coincidence, should not be a matter from human intuition – expert statistical analysis is required", he said.

Richard Gill, an emeritus professor of statistics at Leiden University, and a co-author of the RSS Report in 2022, said "the investigation made mistakes in handling evidence, and that neither the prosecution nor the defence made use of the report's recommendations". Gill said that a 'meaningful analysis,' was not carried out to explore whether or not there was a 'higher rate' of incidents during Letby's shifts than outside them. Gill also raised concerns about the lack of adherence to the rules put down by the Lord Chief Justice for presentation of 'scientific evidence', adding that he supported a 'retrial'. Letby is seeking to challenge her convictions at the Court of Appeal.

Source: The Guardian, 3, October, 2023. Author: Nicola Davies, Science Correspondent.

A corporate manslaughter investigation has been launched into the hospital where killer nurse Lucy Letby murdered seven babies, police have revealed. Officers have said they would focus on the 12 months when Letby committed her appalling crimes at the Countess of Chester Hospital's neonatal unit, between June 2015 and June, 2016. The focus is on 'areas including senior leadership and decision-making'. Cheshire Constabulary, which is carrying out the inquiry, said it was not investigating any individuals in relation to 'gross negligence manslaughter'. Further details have not been released, but it is known that from October, 2015, key members of the hospital's executive team were aware of consultant's fears about

Letby; concerns about 'unnatural events' at the neo-natal unit were raised that June, but at that stage doctors could not believe a member of the medical staff was responsible.

Detective Superintendent Simon Blackwell, strategic lead for 'Operation Hummingbird', the police investigation into Letby, stated: "Following the lengthy trial, subsequent conviction of Lucy Letby, and an assessment by senior investigating officers, I can confirm that Cheshire Constabulary is carrying out an investigation into 'corporate manslaughter' at the Countess of Chester Hospital. We recognise that this investigation will have a significant impact on a number of different stakeholders, including the families in this case, and we are continuing to work alongside and support them during this process."

A father of twins who Letby tried to kill said he hoped there would be 'no hiding place if any criminal wrongdoing is identified'. He said: "We welcome the news of 'corporate manslaughter' proceedings against the trust. Hopefully, now there will be no hiding place for the senior management".

Tim Annett, of Irwin Mitchell, one of the law firms representing the families of the victims' said: "All they want is for no stone to be left unturned. Lessons need to be learned about the early recognition of serious and avoidable harm. It's also vital that, where necessary, appropriate steps are taken to avoid or minimise the risk of future incidents involving the most vulnerable patients". Tony Chambers stepped down as Chief Executive of the hospital trust in September, 2018, two months after Letby was arrested. He said he was 'truly sorry' for what all the families have gone through, and that he intended to 'cooperate fully and openly' with the police investigation.

Jane Tomkinson, acting Chief Executive at the hospital trust, said: "We will be cooperating fully with the investigation so that we can help get the answers that the families and babies affected by this case rightly deserve. It

would not be appropriate for the trust to make any further comment."
Source: Daily Mail, 5, October, 2023. Authors: Richard Marsden and James Tozer.

The Lucy Letby Inquiry will investigate whether NHS staff missed opportunities to stop a neonatal nurse's 'killing spree'. The government listed the 30 key questions it hopes to answer as it aims to put nurses, midwives and doctors under the microscope as well as the wider NHS 'culture'. The inquiry, led by senior judge, Lady Justice Thirlwall, will look at specific concerns raised about Letby and the outcomes of such complaints, and examine whether better security and monitoring could have prevented the murders.

The experiences of parents of babies who died will also come under scrutiny. Following her sentencing, NHS staff claimed their worries were dismissed, with one claiming 'whistleblowers' were 'treated as the problem'. Because it is a statutory inquiry, former and current NHS staff accused of negligence, will be compelled under law to give evidence.
Source: Daily Mail, 20, October, 2023. Author: Elrian Prosser.

Lucy Letby is serving her life sentence in a 'cushy' prison with 24-hour protection, it has emerged. The former nurse who murdered seven babies and tried to kill six more has an en-suite shower, a desk, phone and TV. One source claimed she was being treated with 'kid gloves' because of her notoriety. She has been transferred to privately-run HMP Bronzefield, near Ashford in Surrey, from the tough Low Newton jail near Durham. Letby's treatment is said to be infuriating fellow inmates who have to earn their rights to watch TV, spend their cash and have prison visits. Another source said 'she is in a nice cell on her own'. The facilities at Bronzefield are much nicer than in most jails, because it's privately run. She was held in HMP Bronzefield after being charged in November, 2020 but was moved to HMP New Hall in Wakefield for the trial in

Manchester.

After sentencing, she was taken to Low Newton, located in the village of Brasside near Durham, and was held there in segregation to stop her being attacked by fellow inmates. Letby will remain on suicide watch at HMP Bronzefield. However, this cannot be continued indefinitely 'because it places too great a strain on prison staff'.
Source: Daily Mail, 1 December 2023. Author: Frank Elliott.

Stringent new measures will see deaths from apparently 'natural causes' being checked by a second doctor in a bid to prevent a recurrence of the Harold Shipman or Lucy Letby cases. In an overhaul to how deaths are certified, medical examiners will now scrutinise any deaths that do not involve a coroner. Officials say the move would 'protect the public' and 'strengthen safeguards' in the wake of the Letby baby murders.

A national system to cross-check all deaths was first recommended two decades ago at a public inquiry following the deaths of more than 200 people at the hands of GP Harold Shipman. After a series of delays, ministers have confirmed the reforms to 'help prevent criminal activity', and will come into effect from April 2024. Officials said the changes would see medical examiners scrutinise all deaths in England and Wales not referred to coroners, expanding the system from hospitals to include GPs certifying deaths in the community. For years, Britain's most prolific serial killer, Harold Shipman, was able to escape detection by certifying patients he murdered as having died of 'natural causes', avoiding scrutiny by a coroner.
Source: Daily Mail, 15, December, 2023. Author: Kate Pickles.

An Overview of Corporate Manslaughter and the Case of Lucy Letby

Lucy Letby, the former neonatal nurse was jailed in

August for the murder of seven babies and attempted murder of six others, at the Countess of Chester Hospital. Now Cheshire Police have decided to investigate the hospital for corporate manslaughter, looking at the role of senior leaders in their 'decision making' to determine if any criminality took place. There will be consideration of whether the actions of senior leaders fell below what could be reasonably expected of them, so that Letby was able to murder those seven babies. The offence of 'corporate manslaughter' states that organisations can be responsible for causing the death of individuals where there is a 'serious failing' of a 'duty of care' owed by that organisation, and senior management were 'instrumental in that breach'.

Section 1 (1) of the Corporate Manslaughter and Corporate Homicide Act (2007) outlines the offence. "An organisation to which this section applies is guilty of an offence if the way in which its activities are managed or organised; (a) causes a person's death and (b) amounts to a gross breach of a relevant duty of care owed by the organisation to the deceased".

The elements of the offence are: The defendant must be a qualifying organisation, a corporation, a government department, except for a crown department, a police force, a partnership or trade union or employer's association which is also an employer. A hospital is caught within this definition. The organisation must have owed a relevant duty of care to the deceased. This includes duties owed to employees or other people working for the organisation, or whom they are responsible for the safety of, a duty as an occupier of premises, a duty in connection with the supply of goods or services, commercial activities, construction or maintenance operatives or keeping plant or machinery. The Countess of Chester Hospital did owe a duty of care to the babies in their care in the neonatal unit and to their families.

There must be a gross breach of this duty of care. This must be far below what can reasonably be expected in the circumstances. This gross breach must have come from senior management, who have played a significant role in the decision making or managing, or organising of activities which have led to the event. This may be the most difficult area to prove.

Source: www.tutor2u.net /law/blog. Author: Gemma Shepherd-Etchells, 13, December, 2023.

THE THIRLWALL INQUIRY
Terms of Reference

The inquiry will investigate 3 broad areas:

The experiences of the Countess of Chester Hospital and other relevant NHS service, of all the parents of the babies named in the indictment.

The conduct of those working at the Countess of Chester Hospital, including the board, managers, doctors, nurses and midwives with regard to the actions of Lucy Letby while she was employed there as a neonatal nurse and subsequently including:

(i) Whether suspicions should have been raised earlier, whether Lucy Letby should have been suspended earlier and whether the police and other external bodies should have been informed sooner of suspicions about her.

(ii) The responses to concerns raised about Lucy Letby from those with management responsibilities within the trust.

(iii) Whether the trust's culture, management and governance structures and processes contributed to the failure to protect babies from Lucy Letby.

The effectiveness of NHS management and governance structures and processes, external scrutiny and professional regulation in keeping babies in hospital safe and well looked after, whether changes are necessary and, if so, what they should be, including how accountability of senior managers should be strengthened. This section will include a consideration of NHS culture.

THE LUCY LETBY CASE: LESSONS FOR HEALTH SYSTEMS
Editorial

"Lucy Letby will spend life in prison for murdering seven infants and attempting to kill at least six others during her time as a nurse. Although such a horrifying case is rare, it is not unique. Numerous medical professionals have intentionally killed or harmed patients. Attention is now turning to establishing what exactly happened and what lessons might be learned. An inquiry is underway, but can we expect a strong system of accountability and a cultural shift to result from it?

The inquiry after the Mid-Staffordshire scandal – during which hundreds of patients died in a single hospital over four years due to management-induced systematic failures, led to 290 recommendations and the introduction of the NHS's Duty of Candour. Yet, 10 years after Mid-Staffordshire, and 20 years after the inquiry into Harold Shipman, the UK is trying to understand how top-down systematic failures enabled a medical serial killer to go unchecked. International experience shows that generating solutions is not easy.

Strong vetting processes are important to try to prevent the appointment of those who might harm patients. But how easy is it to detect potential killers? Efforts have been made to build psychological profiles of common traits of medical serial killers, but Letby appeared to be a model nurse, with none of these traits. Recording and flagging a history of malpractice is essential, but it will only work if clinics act responsibly. Niels Hogel, a nurse who killed at least 85 patients in Germany, was sacked from the Oldenburg Clinic following clear indicators that he was harming patients. Rather than go through disciplinary procedures that would remain on his employment record, the clinic gave him a positive reference and he continued his crimes elsewhere.

Whistleblowers are most often the ones to bring medical murderers to light, when colleagues notice excess deaths, odd behaviour, or other patterns of suspicion. But it is hard to be a whistleblower in any context, particularly due to fear of retribution, and especially so in medicine given the extreme stress, busy environment, and the expectations of death in the job. It is vital that their concerns are taken seriously by those in power. In the case of Letby, whistleblowers were reportedly ignored and even made to apologise.

Health-care workers have a moral duty to speak up, but there must be protections that allow them to do so safely. Mortality and morbidity meetings give health-care workers an open environment to discuss deaths and concerning cases to help improve clinical care. However, these meetings lack standardisation and some providers do not attend out of fear of litigation. Health-care workers have even been taken to court for whistleblowing, as was Anne Mitchell, a nurse who was arrested after bringing a misgiving about a colleague to the medical board.

Charles Cullen, a nurse who killed at least 29 patients in the USA, was reported by numerous colleagues at various institutions for drugging patients, but hospital officials did not report his behaviour, even offering him resignation deals or positive references. At the time the state law did not require hospitals to report a nurse under potential investigation, and the National Practitioner Data Bank only collected data on those convicted of a crime. Thus, those in charge lacked the incentive to report Cullen, so instead passed their problem on to others.

In the wake of the Letby case, politicians want to hold NHS managers more accountable with better regulations. These regulations need to stay patient-focused and not just punitive. In for-profit health systems, hospitals are businesses. But even in publicly funded systems like the NHS, repeated rounds of cost-cutting, increased privatisation, and a focus on efficiencies risks undermining the running of hospitals as institutions of care. These pressures, coupled with a focus on a hospital's reputation, are likely to lead to an environment of defensiveness. The idea of a medical professional committing violence against people in their care – often in positions of vulnerability, is difficult to comprehend and there is a feeling of urgency to find solutions. But rushing into regulation and policy can be unwise and unproductive.

A statutory inquiry into the Lucy Letby case is needed to establish what happened and to identify areas to strengthen. There will be no simple remedy. Such inquiries often conclude with the need for a more honest, open, and self-critical hospital environment, but changing the culture of a workplace is not easy in a system that is stressed and stretched thin. Whether health systems – from top to bottom – are making care their priority is judged on actions, not words."

Source: The Lancet, vol 402, September, 2, 2023.

CHAPTER FIVE
Reflections

This final chapter comprises a selection of commentaries and articles on the Letby case in general, and its impact for healthcare in the UK in particular. Taken collectively, these commentaries provide the reader with both a personal and perhaps controversial but thought-provoking overview of the case and its impact on healthcare provision within the UK.

Sir Robert Francis: 'This is Not Just About Lucy Letby – The NHS System Doesn't Value Safety'

"The Patients Association president, who also chaired the inquiry into Mid-Staffs, fears patients are being put at risk by bad management. Sir Robert Francis is the kind of patrician grey-haired chap who gives the establishment a good name. A barrister, King's Counsel, and president of the Patients Association, he's the man we trust to chair big inquires when things go terribly wrong in the NHS. The lessons for the NHS that came out of his epic five-year inquiry into high numbers of deaths in elderly patients at Stafford hospital, enshrined a "duty of candour" in the NHS. His lessons on accountability and culture are taught to all medical students. If ever there was a moment for his cool, experienced head, this is it. This week saw the conviction of Britain's most prolific female serial killer; a nurse whose victims were the most vulnerable patients of all, premature and critically-ill babies.

The perpetrator of these unimaginably awful crimes was Lucy Letby, 33, a nurse at the Countess of Chester Hospital, who worked in the neonatal unit and in neonatal intensive care. After a nine-month trial and six weeks of jury deliberation, she has been found guilty of murdering seven babies and attempting to murder another six. In his closing speech, the prosecuting barrister said: "Letby revelled in what she had done and enjoyed the anguish and distress she had caused". It is expected that Letby will serve a whole-life sentence in prison – not that that will bring back the children who lost their lives, or comfort their grieving parents. And this may not be the full extent of her crimes. Cheshire Police are already pursuing a number of active investigations, including examining 4,000 admissions of babies to neonatal units at the Countess of Chester and Liverpool Women's Hospital, where Letby worked between 2012 and 2016. Consultants on the Countess of Chester unit raised concerns about the unusually high rate of baby deaths, but the hospital was slow to act on their concerns. When "lovely Lucy", as her fellow medics called her, was finally suspended from duty, hospital administrators kept trying to force doctors to reinstate her on the ward, citing "staff shortages".

A BBC investigation found that hospital bosses failed to investigate allegations against Letby and tried to silence doctors. The unit's lead consultant, Dr Stephen Brearey, raised his worries about Letby in October 2015, but no action was taken. It was three years until Letby was arrested, and it took Brearey going to the police as a last resort. Sir Robert, aged 73, has spent his entire career trying to ensure patient safety. How does he think we can stop something like this case happening again? "The first thing to say is to recognise the suffering of the families involved in this shocking tragedy and how awful the staff at the hospital will be feeling, too", he says, when we meet at his chambers, Sergeant's Inn in Fleet Street.

"There needs to be a proper, independent and transparent review of everything that happened as swiftly as possible, but I would say not another public inquiry. We don't need five years of looking at this to come to the same conclusions about putting patient safety at the forefront". He talks about recommendations after previous inquiries for the establishment of independent medical examiners, whose job is to investigate unexplained deaths in hospitals and work with the coroner. "We need to find explanations for startling facts (like babies dying). To do that, we need people who are skilled at investigations and who are independent doctors".

Unfortunately, these are still not in place in the NHS, partly because of costs. Sir Robert intimates that such an external eye could have prevented more deaths in the Letby case. One of the reasons it has taken so long to get verdicts is because it was such a difficult case to prosecute. Letby was cunning at covering her tracks. "It was almost entirely circumstantial evidence, hardly any forensic evidence, lots of clinical evidence relying on recollection which has contributed to the length of the trial", he explains. "There are some learnings about behaviours, particularly about Letby's weird approaches to parents and families after the deaths. But it's difficult to lay down rules and policies because you can't make rules about personalities." "Dr Harold Shipman, the most prolific NHS serial killer, was thought to be a nice, kindly chap, popular with his patients. Some of the most notoriously horrible people can be brilliant surgeons. We need to look at the objective facts and it seems like the consultants who were worried and correlated the deaths with the presence of Letby were looking at objective facts. The explanations are not always sinister", he points out. "Florence Nightingale looked at why people were dying in one ward and not another, it turned out it was because people weren't washing their hands. But we do need to look at the facts and if there are more deaths than usual that needs to be made a priority". This is at the core of Sr Robert's work. "At the heart of this tragic case are concerns raised by doctors about the safety of patients who have died. Whenever that happens, the prime concern in any investigation is to start with the safety of the patient, because if you have concerns about patients then you act urgently.

If you start looking at disputes between individuals, or HR procedures, then you get into trouble, things lag. These insights are hard-won; not just from his decades as a leading medical negligence barrister, but from his epoch-defining inquiry and report into the failures of Mid-Staffordshire NHS Foundation Trust in 2014. It is now a compulsory text in all doctors' training and outlined in detail how up to 1,200 patients died who shouldn't have, because between 2005 and 2008, hospital bosses prioritised "making cutbacks to staffing in services in order to make millions of pounds worth of surpluses".

He made such a name for himself as a champion of patient's safety with the report, that afterwards he became president of the Patients Association, chair of Healthwatch England, and also chaired an NHS review into protecting whistleblowers called the Freedom to Speak Up review. His career has been spent digging deep into how regulators, government, politicians, and administrators in the NHS can fuel care disasters, and exposing how a culture from the Home Secretary downwards can become remote from the reality of service at the front line.

There are obvious parallels between the reluctance of managers to act in the Letby case and the Mid-Staff scandal. Sir Robert points out that in the Mid Staff inquiry, rather than focusing on risks to patients, when it found that the hospital's death rates were significantly higher than they should be, managers "attacked the statistical basis of the data rather than starting with patient safety".

In the Letby trial much was made by the hospital of "staff shortages" as a reason for why Letby needed to be reinstated on the ward (she also brought a grievance procedure against the hospital). Sir Robert sighs. It must be depressing to be like Cassandra, warning of the risks and seeing the same issues recur. "It comes back to the pressures within the NHS system, if you are under pressure from the demands of lots of patients," he says. "Nothing is more testing than looking after intensive care patients when you haven't the staff to do the job. Basically, if there aren't enough staff to run a unit safely, then it should be shut down and patients moved to other hospitals". The Letby trial heard how senior consultants repeatedly raised safety concerns about Letby with hospital management, but that they kept insisting she should be reinstated, the implication being because of staff shortages on the wards (this was found to be the case in a Care Quality Commission report into the unit at the time). If the doctors' warning had been heeded and the hospital had acted sooner, she might have been stopped earlier and lives saved.

Sir Robert shakes his head. The twinkle is in abeyance for now. "I'm afraid in the NHS people are influenced by the systematic pressures put on them to take decisions that in the ideal world they wouldn't take". This is the crux of the matter. "It's a question of priorities", he says. "In the NHS now, there are lots of pressing priorities. The big one is waiting lists which are terrible. It's a problem of excessive demand over supply and that could lead to dire social consequences, which might include the collapse of the service or that the service becomes so ineffective that people look at different ways of doing it".

Sir Robert's view of the series of strikes by junior and consultant doctors should be open to negotiation between the respective parties. When I go to a judge with a big figure for a medical negligence claim it's an opening position. He certainly seems to think there is scope for dialogue. "What the government needs to understand is that this is a question of the working conditions," he says. "When I talk to doctors they say pay matters, but there is just as much that needs to be looked at in terms of working conditions; rostering, burnout, trauma. If that was tackled effectively, they would be less strident about pay. It's as basic as doctors working all night but not being able to get a drink of water, or have a lie-down because those facilities have been withdrawn. Fundamentally, many of the problems in the NHS are down to bad management. I don't think there is anywhere in the private sector that would behave this badly. It's an accident waiting to happen."

He goes on to explain that from his many years of investigating medical negligence it is always when the system gets put under this kind of pressure, that things go wrong. "I am concerned about patient safety because when things get this bad there is a lack of speaking up; pressure on staff just to do the work, even when that becomes impossible, when junior doctors are so tired they can't drive home. All NHS staff feel a moral imperative to look after patients, but they can't when just doing their jobs is such a threat to their wellbeing. "It's not about snowflakes, or not being resilient. Anyone who has done five years of basic training as a doctor is resilient. It becomes worrying to me when it becomes normal just to put up with it. You don't want to let your colleagues down so you keep going, and then junior doctors have concerns about patient safety or around practices of senior colleagues and don't speak up. That's dangerous and puts patients at an unacceptable risk."

Sir Robert points to an 11.3 per cent increase in serious patient safety incidents in the past six months. That's 2,435,8000 incidents; "and each of those two-and-a-half million is a person; your mum, your wife, your baby, your father, these are just the ones that are reported".

Yet despite Letby and the increase in unsafe incidents, Sir Robert sounds a comforting note by saying that things are way better than they used to be. "When I started working in medical negligence as a young lawyer in the 1970s such claims hardly existed because no doctor would give evidence against another. I've seen a massive shift in terms of claims and taking responsibility. We hear about what has gone wrong more. The duty of candour (this enshrines the notion that doctors and nurses must tell the truth about what happened to preserve patient safety) that I talked about in the Mid-Staffs report is there. I do hear that NHS workers now feel a protection in terms of speaking up when things go wrong. We saw this in the Letby case, when the neonatal consultants did raise the alarm, so what needs to be done? There is a retention crisis. A General Medical Council survey showed that 40 per cent of NHS workers are thinking of leaving, 60 per cent say they can't cope and it's getting worse all the time".

But Sir Robert warns against more NHS reorganisation and targets. "It was a big reorganisation that led to Mid-Staffs and the negative culture. I will never forget a woman in that inquiry telling me how she arrived to find her elderly mother naked, barely covered with a sheet, in full view of the corridor, and with faeces dried on to her sheets, which were also soaked in urine. The worst thing about that was that she'd been like that for a long time, many people had seen it and done nothing. That is when an institutional culture becomes dangerous." I ask what other cases haunt him. "I'll never forget the story of a woman with a broken hip who came to A & E, she was diabetic and it said clearly on her notes: needs insulin. But 11 days later she had been given no insulin and she died in the hospital. It's the thoughtlessness behind lots of these unsafe practices which leads to harm and death. When things go wrong it is not only about rogue individuals like Letby or Shipman, but a system which doesn't value safety and prioritise patients. It's when people aren't listened to, that's when bad things happen."

Does he feel optimistic about the future of the NHS, or is it broken beyond repair? "No", he replies to the latter with passion. I believe him. As long as the NHS has wise critical friends such as Sir Robert, it stands a chance of staying the distance. Sir Robert Frances who led inquiries into appalling suffering endured by hundreds of patients as managers obsessed with targets ignored staff concerns said: "My initial thoughts were in favour of a non-statutory inquiry simply because you could get on with it, the lessons to be learned could be found quickly. The disadvantage is you can't compel people to give evidence, it's not given on oath and so on". He said the government should "appoint a chair of the inquiry in a non-statutory way but task that chair with consulting those concerned, particularly bereaved families, about terms of reference and whether it should be statutory or non-statutory."

Francis said: "I had in Mid-Staff the experience of both (statutory and non-statutory) and I thought that worked quite well, starting with the non-statutory which allowed me much more flexibility in how to go about investigating, talking to people, learning how things happened, and then having a statutory inquiry looking at the wider system picture". He suggested the need for a police investigation into other cases would delay some elements of the inquiry, meaning these could potentially be the subject of a wider statutory probe later. "What happened in (the) hospital, what concerns were raised and how they were dealt with could be the start whereas the wider picture could follow." He said, "There is time to do a consultation and perhaps work out a structure of what can be done sooner and what would wait until more is known."
Source: The Telegraph, 19 August 2023. Author: Eleanor Mills.

Analysis

"Shortly after Grantham Hospital nurse Beverly Allitt was sent to prison in 1993 for killing four babies, I was asked to assess a nurse in the hospital in which I worked. It was feared she shared some of Allitt's characteristics, including a tendency to turn up in hospital casualty departments with made-up complaints. It was an anxiety-provoking problem for me. There was no evidence that the individual I was assessing had done anything wrong on her ward, but what if I passed her as fit and she went on to kill? In the end, I concluded that there was nothing to be done except to watch closely for anything untoward and several years later, I am very relieved to say, there had been no suspicious incidents. This illustrates the difficulty of picking out monsters in advance of other crimes being uncovered. In the case of Lucy Letby, of course, many warning signs were either missed or dismissed. But she was caught in the end and now faces life in prison.

As a former prison psychiatrist, I know the first task of the governor of the prison where she'll serve her sentence, will be to protect her both from herself and the other inmates. Every prisoner who has been found guilty of murder is automatically put on suicide watch, on the reasonable supposition that all those who face decades in prison may be tempted to kill themselves. Suicide watch takes a number of different forms, from CCTV cameras, or direct supervision by a dedicated prison officer, to a system of regular checks, every five, ten or 15 minutes.

As hanging, by far the most common way to commit suicide in prison, is one of the quickest means of ending it all, periodic checks can be largely ineffective, as the death of the billionaire paedophile Jeffrey Epstein in New York's Metropolitan Correctional Centre proved. But even direct observation is not infallible. I once knew a man who cut his throat while he was being supervised not by one, but by two officers. Other prisoners aware of his intention to harm himself, had smuggled razor blades into his cell by secreting them in his food. Lucy Letby will long remain a suicide risk, however she appears to the staff. The risk is greatest early in a sentence, but it never disappears entirely, and staff will be only too aware that they will be heavily criticised if such a prominent prisoner were to take her own life. A suicide watch cannot be continued indefinitely however, certainly not for years or decades, as it places too great a strain on the prison staff. It is a matter of judgement when a watch is lifted, and it is not a precise science.

Take the case of the serial killer, Fred West, who hanged himself in HMP Birmingham when I worked there in the mid-1990s. He was able to do this because, after serving months on remand, he appeared cheerful enough to no longer require constant surveillance. Likewise, Dr Harold Shipman at HMP Wakefield, nine years later.

But two high-profile female inmates coped in the end much better with their time in prison. Moors Murderer Myra Hindley, who died in 2002, and Fred's wife Rosemary West, two of the most notorious British female serial killers, both appear to have become 'queen bees' on their wings. West even shared recipes for 'Victoria sponge' with her fellow inmates. 'People on the outside probably think Rose West is banged up in one of those bare cells, like the ones you see on TV', said one of the prison sources. 'But let me tell you it's nothing like it. Her life is about as good as it gets in prison. In fact, it's probably better than for some of your readers on the outside'.

On the face of it, this is unjust. Such people do not deserve a relaxed and pleasant existence, but the system in a civilised society can deliberately inflict misery and hardship for decades on end. Lucy Letby will be a possible target for the rest of her life. She will live in fear of becoming a victim of a murderous attack by other prisoners, some of whom like nothing more than to be the agents of an avenging justice. It may come as a surprise to hear that many prisoners are far from liberal when it comes to sentencing, and a good number of them believe in the death penalty, at least for certain crimes, such as the killing of children.

Rose West was moved to Durham from HMP Bronzefield in Ashford, Middlesex, where Letby has been serving her time on remand, after prisoners were found to be plotting to batter her with pool balls. Letby will, of course, also be the subject of a battery of psychological enquiries and report, and will become the 'patient' of various would-be therapists and healers, whether she wants it or not. Her biography will be gone through with a fine-tooth comb. The object of doing this will be to find an explanation for her actions, with a view to preventing similar incidents in the future.

One of the problems will be that psychopaths of above a certain level of intelligence are often more than a match for the doctors, psychologists and social workers with whom they are confronted. Letby is likely to remain at Bronzefield, for the short term at least. On its website, Bronzefield boasts of its progressive attitude to rehabilitation. But it is difficult to see how they can be relevant in a case such as Letby's. Given the gravity of her crimes, she will, or should, spend the rest of her life in prison. No psychiatrist will ever penetrate that earpiece of innocent denial to discern what drove her to kill."

Source: Daily Mail, 21 April 2023. Author: Dr Anthony Daniels, Former Prison Psychiatrist.

The Grotesque Deeds of this Angel of Death Expose Yet Again, the Culture of Denial, Delay and Secrecy that Scars the NHS

"Stephen Brearey, lead consultant in the unit which in Lucy Letby murdered seven babies and tried to kill seven more has raised an important question. Why, he asks, can doctor and nurses be held accountable by regulations covering medical practitioners, yet some senior managers face minimal governance, and are able to swan off to other highly paid jobs, even if their careers appear to have been beset by tragedy and scandal? Brearey, who first raised the alarm about Letby almost two years before police were finally called in, alleges managers were more worried about their reputation than the safety of their smallest patients, leaving 'whistleblowing' doctors feeling they were under attack, though some managers dispute this.

But the truth is politicians have signally failed to heed the lessons of series of fatal health scandals. Instead of action, there has been hollow talk of learning from tragedy, along with shallow pledges of reform and spewed platitudes about the preciousness of the NHS, even as the most vulnerable patients continue to be betrayed.

This week, Peter Furnes, a former president of the Royal College of Pathologists, pointed out that many of Letby's victims might have been saved if ministers had not delayed a key recommendation from the Harold Shipman inquiry 20 years ago. The probe into more than 200 patients killed by the GP called for medical scrutiny of any death that did not involve a coroner. Yet, astonishingly, hospitals began to introduce this practice only four years ago after Letby had committed her vile crimes. A statutory system will not start until next year.

It is, as one grieving mother told the court this week, 'shocking that someone as evil as Letby exists'. Her colleagues could never have imagined one of their team might have been a serial killer, despite the rise in deaths of newborns. But it is beyond disturbing that, after doctors pieced together the evidence that Letby's presence was the sinister link between deaths, their concerns were dismissed.

Yet again, seemingly indifferent health chiefs are lurking in the shadows of tragedy. Once more, we see how denial and obfuscation corrode the sacred NHS. Politicians talk of transparency, health chiefs create codes of conduct, managers claim to be open, but when mistakes are made and systems fail, the reaction is all too often to crush complaints and sweep concerns under the carpet. On many previous occasions, staff, patients or bereaved families have raised alarms only to be bullied, gagged or ignored.

Doctors accused the Countess of Chester NHS Trust of negligence in its failure to address their concerns. One told the court they were 'instructed not to make a fuss, while the medical director failed to respond to a request for a meeting about the spike in baby deaths for three months. They say executives backed Letby's protestations of victimisation after inadequate enquiries, even though one doctor reportedly told his manager they were 'harbouring a murderer'. Unbelievably, it was they who were ordered to apologise to Letby, and even to attend mediation sessions.

This pattern of behaviour by senior managers certainly led to more deaths. "I genuinely believe that there are four or five babies who could be going to school now who aren't", consultant Ravi Jayaram told ITV News. The issues will no doubt be examined by the inquiry announced last week by Health Secretary, Steve Barclay, and it is critical that he puts it on a statutory basis to force witnesses to participate.

Yet, it is hard to be optimistic that the findings will jolt the system sufficiently to cure it of its sickness and solve the shameful bureaucratic failings. There have been at least 100 such investigations into families in NHS care over the past half century, and many of these highly forensic investigations, carried out by diligent experts, have come to startlingly similar conclusions. They have warned about defensive management, dire communication and dysfunctional bureaucracy. Again and again, they have pleaded for whistleblowers to be taken seriously rather than be stigmatised by intransigent health chefs or simply ignored. Yet far too little has changed.

The first modern health care inquiry led by the lawyer, Geoffrey Howe, who later became Chancellor of the Exchequer under Margaret Thatcher, was into the abusive treatment of people with learning disabilities at Ely psychiatric hospital in Cardiff. This influential 1969 report, sparked by public outrage after investigative journalists exposed a culture of cruelty, led to the establishment of the first NHS inspectorate. Labour ministers praised the inquiry, after it found 'it's biggest single deficiency' was the 'odious and alarming' targeting of whistleblowers. They stressed the need for medical staff to be able to raise concerns in a supportive culture.

Since then, a string of scandals, including the Shipman murders, has underlined the importance of listening to whistleblowers rather than closing ranks. Yet all too often thy are still treated with contempt. Anaesthetist, Stephen Bolsin, said he was driven out of the country to Australia after his eight-year struggle to lift the lid on cardiac surgery failures that led to possibly 170 avoidable deaths of children in the 1990s at Bristol Royal Infirmary.

The Francis Inquiry into the Mid-Staff catastrophe, where hundreds of patients died due to sordid neglect in two Mid-Staffordshire hospitals, examined what was seen as the worst hospital care failure in NHS history. It revealed 'a culture of fear in which staff did not feel able to report concerns, a culture of secrecy in which the trust's board ignored its patients and a culture of bullying, which prevented people from doing their jobs properly.

The landmark report called for this to be replaced by 'openness, honesty and transparency, where the only fear is the failure to uphold fundamental standards and the caring culture'. This sparked new efforts to protect whistleblowers. Yet the failure to do so was apparent again last year in the devastating final report into the Shrewsbury maternity scandal, where 201 babies and nine mothers may have needlessly died. One Shrewsbury obstetrician talked about a 'culture of fear' that left staff scared to speak out for 'risk of victimisation' His words echoing precisely the problem unearthed both by the Francis Inquiry, and the findings of the Howe Report more than half a century earlier.

Even now, journalists keep exposing the shocking abuse of people with autism and learning difficulties locked up in psychiatric hospitals. The NHS relies on fallible human beings, so it needs a culture in which those who expose problems are not blamed, a culture that rests on truth and transparency, revolves around patient safety, and encourages whistleblowers rather than thwarting them. Letby, like her fellow mass-murderer, Shipman, was an aberration among these cases; a serial killer in nurse's uniform, on a malevolent mission to inflict misery on families who should have been enjoying the most magical of life's experiences. She alone carries the cross of her evil. We cannot predict the inquiry's conclusions, but the grotesque deeds of this angel of death expose again the disturbing culture of denial, delay and secrecy that scars the NHS with such horrific consequences."

Source: Daily Mail, 23, April, 2023. Author: Ian Birrell. The author of this article has campaigned on health service failures for 15 years.

Mind of a Murderer

"The closest Lucy Letby is ever to come to a confession of her depraved thoughts and intentions are the Post-it notes crammed with her minute scrawls. Detectives have suggested that these scraps of evidence were left for police to find in her semi-detached house in Westbourne Road, Chester, in an oblique but deliberate attempt to bring her spree of killing to an end. Though I have great respect for the police force's painstaking case against this heinous killer, I can't agree with their interpretation. These scribbled notes are, quite simply, a glimpse into Lucy Letby's psyche.

As a forensic psychiatrist, it's my job to treat and rehabilitate what some call the 'criminally insane', many of whom assault, rob rape and even kill. My work takes me to high-security prisons and securely locked hospital wards across the country, as well as inside courtrooms giving evidence as an 'expert' witness. In my career I have examined four women who murdered babies. All of them were suffering from psychotic delusions so severe that their grasp on reality had broken.

That is not what we're seeing in these Post-it notes. There is no evidence here of a mental illness so serious that it might reduce Letby's criminal culpability. What does leap out at me are the expressions of self-hatred, guilt, shame and self-loathing, along with a low self-confidence, what psychiatrists call 'negative cognitions.'. We see it in phrases such as: 'I don't deserve Mum and Dad', 'Hate myself', 'I am a horrible evil person', 'I don't deserve to live', and 'The world is better off without me'. Down the right-hand side of the green note she has added annotations in capital letters: 'NO HOPE', 'DESPAIR', 'PANIC', 'FEAR', 'LOST'.

Two overlapping reasons combine to explain such outbursts. The first, though this in no way diminishes the wickedness of her actions, is a modicum of awareness that what she has done is too terrible to imagine. She says: "There are no words. I am an awful person – I pay every day for that". A tiny part of her, though it conflicted with what she was actually doing to those babes, appears to be feeling guilt. Perhaps that is why the words are squeezed into such small pieces of paper. As well as self-pity, they represent her conscience, and that was very limited in scope and size.

There wasn't enough guilt to stop her from continuing to kill, nor enough to make her admit what she had done during the trial. But that doesn't mean there wasn't a sliver of her subconscious mind that was conflicted. The second possible explanation is the obvious signs of depression and anxiety in these frantic scribbles. Such negative thoughts are a common expression of depression. It is quite likely that she didn't know what was going to happen when she started writing on these Post-it notes. One of them is headed 'Not Good Enough', and she might have begun with the intention of just jotting a couple of thoughts down, before they exploded out of her in this chaotic and possibly cathartic rush.

The words that run into each other, the repeated loops and letters, the "HELP" and "HATE" overlaid in heavy black writing, and the overall intensity, are all signs of a mind in turmoil. But even if she was suffering from depression, the symptoms were not severe enough to stop her from functioning normally. To colleagues at the hospital, she didn't seem unduly stressed in her high-pressure role of supposedly caring for babes on the 'precipice' of death. Some of the thoughts are contradictory. She writes:" I haven't done anything wrong." But a few lines later, she admits" I AM EVIL. I DID THIS". The battle between right and wrong is palpable. We, of course, know which won. I have seen cases where people have committed crimes and later convinced themselves that the actions they remember never actually happened. That's not true of Lucy Letby. She knows deep down that she murdered those seven babies and harmed many more, but she is deeply invested in her own lies, and the idea of her innocence so completely, that she feels aggrieved that anyone could doubt her words.

This is a well-known contradiction in many people who commit less serious crimes, such as financial fraud; they have got away with it for so long, although they know they are guilty, they feel it's unreasonable for anyone to accuse them. It's a kind of 'narcissistic entitlement', of believing they're above the law. There is also evidence of clinical psychopathy. In other words, she is a remorseless killer, guilty of unprecedented crimes, but that does not mean she automatically has all the typical traits of a 'psychopath'. Some of the common ones appear to be missing. She was not sexually promiscuous for example, nor does she seem to be a generally parasitic and deceptive individual across every aspect of her life.

Of course, she lied consistently to police and throughout her trial, but there was a rational reason for that. She was trying to hide her crimes. There's no sign in these notes that she lies for the sake of it, or that she weaves a fantasy world. She may understand, at least, as a plain fact, that what she did was 'morally repugnant'. We call that 'cognitive empathy', knowing when other people are suffering. But clearly, she lacks all 'emotive empathy' and cannot feel what others are feeling. Their pain does not make her suffer. In fact, she gains some enjoyment from it.

I've spent hours trying to understand Letby's motives. Many experts have seized on one sentence in particular: "I killed them on purpose because I'm not good enough to care for them". But it is a mistake to take that at face value. It is not an explanation, only an outburst of 'self-pity'.

Her true motivations, I believe are power, control, and the thrill of being around the grieving process. There's evidence of vitriolic anger or jealousy towards the happy family unit, expressed in the words: "I'll never know what it's like to have a family". We know that Letby wanted to be present when patients were overwhelmed by grief, even when the dead babies had not been her own patients. She even sent one family a sympathy card after murdering their premature baby. Clearly, there is a morbid urge to feed off their pain. Yet, she is not blind to emotion. In some of her scribblings, particularly on a paper torn from a note-book, and covered closely on both sides, Letby repeatedly writes the names of her cats, Trigger and Smudge. The animals were a way for her to show affection and emotion while remaining completely in control. Lucy Letby is the most extraordinary and unique clinical case I have encountered. From what we know of her life before concerns began to be raised about the baby deaths, nothing about her struck people as strange. She was not aggressive or impulsive, paranoid or cantankerous. Colleagues thought of her as friendly and approachable, diligent as well as competent. I doubt whether we will ever fully understand her. Because she will never leave prison, she is unlikely to get the kind of intensive psychiatric support that could lead to real remorse."

Source: *Daily Mail, 23, August, 2023. Author: Dr Sohom Das, Forensic Psychiatrist.*

Letby Disaster Epitomises Flaws in the NHS

"The tragic events of the Lucy Letby case show the urgent need for an independent regulator for non-clinical managers. It is impossible to make sense of the awful, appalling crimes in the Lucy Letby case. Words cannot begin to describe how distressing the details of these crimes are, nor the anguish for the families of the victims, and all the healthcare staff involved that will haunt them forever. These horrific events will sit uncomfortably with doctors across the country who are universally asking, 'how on earth did it take over a year after repeated concerns and warnings were raised by consultants, before any criminal investigation into the deaths was ordered?'

This is the unbelievable worst-case scenario that has turned out to be true. It epitomises systematic flaws and failing in our health service where doctors and healthcare staff are not appreciated for flagging that there is something seriously wrong happening to their patients. This must be the last straw and the turning point in a shameful and toxic culture.

As doctors, we are obliged to report concerns when we identify risks to patient safety, yet there is a sense felt by many of my colleagues that in doing so, they face resentment and are seen as the problematic, questioning ones who just think they know best. When it comes to the science, evidence and expertise behind patient care, we do often know more than most, and critically, are trained to seek out – and keep seeking out – explanations for when outcomes are not as expected. We have a duty to understand what may have gone wrong and what could be done differently in future for the next patients in similar circumstances. Too often our voices are stifled because truths are uncomfortable, or may carry potential reputational damage for an individual or organisation – or government. Ironically, the most damage comes from not listening to these concerns, the sometimes-fatal consequences of delayed investigations and late interventions. The lack of senior doctors on executive and board positions in NHS organisations is just one example of how valuable independent representation on a clinical level is absent.

This case raises serious questions about how healthcare providers are governed. The board claimed that they were misled because they didn't have specialist medical knowledge to assess what was being raised. It is unacceptable that there was no way for senior doctors to raise serious concerns directly with non-executive directors. The case of Lucy Letby shows the devastating and unspeakable harm that can come from doctors and healthcare staff feeling worried or even threatened for raising patient safety concerns. Ultimately, doctors who were prevented from raising concerns with the police owing to the potential reputational damage to the trust, prevailed.

The threat of a vexatious GMC referral and investigation can take an enormous toll on a doctor's mental health and wellbeing. The gravity of such a threat should not be underestimated. A GMC investigation can end a career and seems to be being deliberately used as a deterrent to stop doctors from raising or continuing to pursue legitimate patient safety concerns across the UK.

Of course, this case is not the first where the concerns of senior doctors were poorly handled or dismissed and serious failures have occurred as a result. As far back as 2013, Sir Robert Francs KC published a report outlining the causes of serious failures in care at Mid Staffordshire NHS Foundation Trust, identifying a range of issues of medical negligence, poor culture and lack of transparency.

For years, the BMA has campaigned for a change in the culture of blame and suspicion within the NHS and has long called for non-clinical managers to be regulated. The Letby case shows we are a long way off the change that is needed. We need a regulatory mechanism for holding senior non-clinical managers to account, in line with the way clinical staff are held to account by our regulator. The inquiry into the murder of innocent babies in Chester must be put on a full statutory footing with the powers to compel witnesses to attend. Unless those involved are made to provide evidence, the government will be perpetuating the view that non-medical managers are beyond accountability.

Importantly, any inquiry must identify any instances where doctors were badly treated for raising safety concerns, including consideration of threats of referrals to the GMC. It must offer solutions that increases the likelihood of openness, transparency and an NHS that will act when there are safety issues. The BMA will continue to stand by doctors who bravely speak out and challenge threats to patient care. The current whistleblowing protections also need legislative reform – too often cases fail not because the safety concern wasn't valid, but because the legal process relies on causation between raising a protected disclosure and subsequent detriment, an incredibly high threshold. Doctors need assurance that their concerns will be listened to and taken seriously, but patients must be in a position where they feel heard and listened to as well. We cannot allow something like this to ever happen again, we owe it to these babies whose lives have been taken so cruelly"

Source: www.bma.org.uk/news/. January 26 2024. Author: Phil Banfield. BMA Council Chairman.

Unravelling the Tangle of Science and Justice in the Lucy Letby Case.

"In the sombre chambers of legal scrutiny, where the gavels' echoes meet the silent hum of laboratory instruments, the case of Lucy Letby emerges as a profound confluence of science and law. Letby, a former nurse, faced the gravest of accusations – murder and attempted murder of infant under her care. The complexity of her case and the recent denial of her leave to appeal, cast a sharp light on the pivotal role that scientific evidence play in the courts of justice. The saga of Letby's trial and conviction weaves a narrative, rich with medical records, text messages, and the haunting prose of personal diaries. It raises a curtain on the unsettling theatre where scientific evidence can be both star and understudy, pivotal yet at times enigmatic in its role. The subsequent denial of her appeal spotlights an uphill battle though the legal system – a system where the very evidence that can exonerate can also condemn. As we embark on this exploration, we delve into the heart of the matter – the reliability of scientific evidence in the pursuit of justice. For in the quest to uncover the truth, the scales of justice must balance the weighty implications of scientific interpretation against the fundamental principles of the legal process.

The Questionable Reliability of Scientific Evidence

Within the stark walls of a courtroom, scientific evidence is often revered as the bedrock of truth. Yet, in the trial of Lucy Letby, it became apparent that even the bedrock can crumble under the scrutiny of doubt and the absence of certainty. The evidence presented a melange of medical records, text messages and handwritten notes, which was wielded with the intent to form an unbreakable chain of guilt.

However, the links of this chain were forged in the fires of interpretation, expert opinion, and contested reliability. The scientific evidence hinged on a few pivotal tests and the implications drawn from them. Blood tests and x-rays stood at the forefront, while the vast and nuanced realm of neonatal physiology lingered in the shadows, its complexity reduced to oversimplified narratives. The defence's strategy to navigate this realm was questioned, not merely for its execution but for the experts they chose, or failed to retain, to challenge the prosecution's case. The result was a narrative that, while legally compelling, left a trail of scientific ambiguity.

As we scrutinise the evidence further, the reliability of these scientific interpretations must be interrogated. The court, a place where clarity is sought amidst the chaos of human affairs, was left to ponder the reliability of expert testimonies, the veracity of amended medical records, and the implications of personal diaries. It was a scenario where the science was as much on trial as the accused herself.

The reliance on expert witnesses who brought their interpretations to the stand, further muddied the waters. In such complex medical cases, where every symptom and test result can be seen through multiple lenses, the expertise and biases of the witnesses can tilt the scales subtly yet significantly. This reliance on subjective interpretation, where definitive scientific consensus is lacking, begs the question – how does one distinguish between evidence and inference, fact and fiction?

Defence Strategy and Legal Team Dynamics

In the intricate dance of courtroom battles, the defence's choreography is as critical as the evidence at hand. For Lucy Letby, whose freedom lay in the balance, Letby's decision to stay with the same legal team that presided over the original case has been met with scrutiny. The success of a defence often hinges on the ability to present a robust counter-narrative to the prosecution's claims, especially in cases steeped in scientific complexity. The choice to retain or replace legal representation is not merely a matter of loyalty or continuity but a strategic consideration of expertise, perspective, and the adeptness at navigating scientific nuances in a legal framework.

The legal team's handling – or alleged mishandling – of expert testimony played a pivotal role. The jury's perception of the evidence is shaped by how confidently and convincingly experts can deconstruct the prosecution's arguments and present alternative interpretations. The failure to effectively challenge the prosecution's scientific assertions could suggest a missed opportunity to introduce reasonable doubt into the minds of the jurors. In the realm of medical legal cases, where the details are dense and the stakes are high, the ability to provide complex information into understandable arguments is paramount.

The strategic missteps alleged against Letby's defence raise critical questions about the role and responsibility of legal teams in ensuring that scientific evidence is thoroughly and accurately scrutinised. As we reflect on the implications of their approach, it becomes apparent that the outcome of the trial can be as much about the narrative constructed in the courtroom as the facts themselves. In the end, it is a narrative that must be carefully crafted, with each piece of evidence and testimony meticulously analysed and positioned for maximum impact.

Role and Function of the Criminal Cases Review Commission, (CCRC)

In the labyrinth of the legal system, where the echoes of verdicts past reverberate through the stone-clad halls of justice, the Criminal Cases Review Commission (CCRC) stands as a beacon of hope for those contesting the finality of a conviction. The CCRC, an independent body with the power to send cases back to the Court of Appeal, represents a critical juncture in the appellate landscape, a place where cases are re-examined under the lens of fresh evidence or new legal arguments.

For individuals like Lucy Letby, whose appeals have stumbled against the formidable walls of judicial decision, the CCRC offers a potential path forward. The Commission's role is not to determine guilt or innocence, but to assess whether there is a 'real possibility' that a conviction would not be upheld if it were subjected to a fresh appeal. The CCRC steps in where traditional appeal routes have been exhausted or have failed to recognise the merits of a case, scrutinising the legal and evidential tapestry of a conviction to ensure that no stone is left unturned.

The historical performance of the CCR reveals a limited landscape of exonerations. Since its inception in April 1997, the CCRC has received almost 29,000 applications, and, of these, it has referred 797 back to the Court of Appeal. These referrals have resulted in 542 convictions being quashed – an impermissibly small number given that many of these cases do not involve serious crimes. The fact that only 18% of applications to the CCRC result in an exoneration is in stark contrast to the scores of exonerations that have been achieved in the US over the same period, and for serious criminal cases. It is estimated that the wrongful conviction rate in the US is around 11% of all convictions.

Letby's case, set against the stark backdrop of these statistics, underscores the gravity of the CCRC's potential intervention. The commission's review could be instrumental in re-evaluating the scientific evidence that formed the basis of her conviction. It stands as a gatekeeper to a fresh appellate examination and perhaps, to a different conclusion.

The Criteria for CCRC Review Under Section 13

The Criminal Cases Review Commission's (CCRC) authority to breathe new life into a seemingly concluded case is enshrined in Section 13 of the Criminal Appeal Act. This legislative cornerstone dictates that the CCRC can refer a case back to the Court of Appeal only under stringent conditions, ensuring that only those cases with a substantive claim of wrongful conviction are reconsidered. First and foremost, the CCRC must determine that there is a 'real possibility' that the original conviction would not be upheld if re-examined. This possibility must be grounded in new evidence or arguments that have not been previously raised in court – evidence that could potentially unravel the fabric of the prosecution's case.

For Lucy Letby, this means that her legal team must unearth fresh evidence or legal arguments that were not considered during the trial or previous appeal. The significance of this is monumental, for it is not enough to simply restate previous claims, there must be a new narrative, a new angle that casts doubt on the integrity of the original conviction.

The intricate journey of a CCRC review is a labyrinth of legal scrutiny, where each turn unveils another layer of examination. Section 13 serves as the map through this labyrinth, guiding the CCRC's hand as it traces the lines of legal and factual relevance, ensuring that justice is not just a result, but a process, an ongoing quest for truth, untainted by oversight or error.

Next Steps for Lucy Letby and her Legal Team

The journey for Lucy Letby, in the wake of her failed appeal, now winds through the corridors of the Criminal Cases Review Commission (CCRC), where new strategies must be conceived and pursued. The task ahead is clear; to unearth new evidence or construct novel legal arguments that could shift the tides in her favour. For Letby's legal team, the strategic imperative is to meticulously comb through the case's history, to challenge every test, every expert opinion, and every piece of evidence presented. They must seek out the overlooked detail, the expert who was never consulted, the test that was never performed. It is a race against the clock to gather new findings that might illuminate paths not previously taken.

This rigorous process requires a careful re-examination of the scientific evidence that led to Letby's conviction. The team must seek out independent experts to re-analyse the medical data, to challenge the conclusions drawn, and to offer alternative interpretations that might suggest a different narrative. Each step must be calibrated to demonstrate the 'real possibility' of a different outcome, a standard set forth by Section 13 of the Criminal Appeal Act. Moreover, the team must engage in a thorough review of procedural aspects, ensuring that no legal stone is left unturned. Any procedural misstep could be the key to unlocking a CCRC review.

The path forward is arduous and fraught with challenge. Yet, it is a necessary traverse to ensure that justice, in its trust form, is served. For Lucy Letby, the fight for a new appeal is more than a legal battle, it is the quest for a second chance, a chance that lies in the hand of her legal team and their ability to navigate the intricate maze of the CCRC's review process.

The Pursuit of Justice in the Shadows of Doubt

The case of Lucy Letby, marked by the intersection of law and complex scientific evidence, underscores the profound challenges faced in the quest for justice. As Letby's path now leads to the door of the Criminal Cases Review Commission (CCRC), her case serves as a poignant reminder of the critical importance of rigour, diligence, and the open-minded revaluation of evidence in the legal process.

The journey ahead, fraught with the need for new evidence or arguments, reflect the daunting hurdles that individuals in Letby's position must overcome. Yet, it also highlights the essential role of entities like the CCRC in safeguarding the integrity of justice, ensuring that every conviction stands the test of thorough scrutiny and that the scales of justice remain balanced in the face of evolving evidence and perspectives.

As we reflect on the broader implications of Letby's case, it becomes clear that the intersection of science and law is a frontier of both challenge and opportunity. It is a domain where the pursuit of truth requires not only the application of legal principles but also an understanding of the nuanced, often complex nature of scientific evidence. It is here, in the meticulous examination of every piece of evidence and every legal argument, that the potential for miscarriages of justice can be addressed and, ultimately, rectified.

In the end, Letby's ongoing struggle for appeal is emblematic of the broader quest for justice faced by many. It is a quest that demands persistence, a commitment to uncovering the truth, and an unwavering belief in the principles of fairness and justice that underpin our legal system. As this case continues to unfold, it serves as a testament to the enduring importance of these principles and to the hope that, even in the face of uncertainty and doubt, justice will prevail."

Source: www.scienceontrial.com/post. 31 January 2024.

WRONGFUL CONVICTIONS REPORT
Lucy Letby – Serial Baby Killer or Wrongfully Convicted Nurse?

An interview with Dr Scott McLachlan by Norman Fenton, raises much doubt about Lucy Letby's guilt, and is part of a report that takes the lid off the most sensational multiple death case in the UK.

"After her conviction for killing seven babies and attempted murder of ten others, nurse Lucy Letby, 33, is expected to spend the rest of her life in prison. The media whipped up such a public frenzy that she would be safer inside. But as some legal commentators argue, her trial was a farce. Is Letby the fall girl for a corrupt system, in which doctors made serious errors and found a convenient scapegoat? The crimes were committed from June 2015 to June 2016, at the neonatal unit at the Countess of Chester Hospital. The impression given is that an exceptional number of babies died during this period, but there were contributory factors unrelated to nursing care, and the peak of infant mortality at the unit occurred in 2019, long after Letby had left.

Almost everyone who knows of Letby's case has only heard the official story of a prolific serial killer punished for unconscionable evil. But in an interview with Norman Fenton, statistician at Queen Mary, University of London, Scott Mc Lachan doubted that any justice was served. A lecturer in applied health technology at King's College, London, Mc Lachan as both nursing and legal qualifications. He has meticulously studied the evidence presented in court, revealing misleading use of data and omission of crucial information.

Of critical importance to the guilty verdict was a chart showing which nurses were on duty at the time of baby collapse and deaths. It looks damning; in every case, Letby was there. But this was horribly misleading; other casualties occurred when Letby was off duty, but these were not considered in court. Data from a freedom of information request to the hospital, showed that 31 infants died in the 12-month period of Letby's adjudged crimes, yet 23 of these were excluded from the trial. Of the eight deaths for which Letby was believed culpable, one case was dropped. In other words, Letby was implicated by circular logic; deaths happened when she was on the unit, so she must have caused them. According to Mc Lachan, various other factors could have caused an elevation in mortality. The neonatal unit had been upgraded, enabling it to provide for premature babies who, previously would have gone to a specialist unit. There was a problem with the plumbing; sewage pipes leaked, risking contamination of the water supply. Mc Lachan suggested that bacterial infection could have been the cause of air in the bloodstream and organs of babies, rather than injection by Letby which nobody witnessed. The role and responsibility of doctors was strangely marginalised in the proceedings. Why weren't they cross-tabulated by infant injury?

Dr Gibbs, the unit consultant, had one foot in the door of retirement at the time of the incidents, and lineal decisions were increasingly taken by the registrar and junior doctors. As McLachan described, inexperienced trainees were performing skilled procedures such as umbilical venous catheterisation, which should be supervised on the first three or more occasions. Sometimes a junior doctor made multiple unsuccessful insertions, raising the risk of infection. Letby was reported to police by consultants, after a critical report about the unit by the Royal College of Paediatrics and Child Health, despite no concerns being raised by Letby's nursing colleagues at the time. Perhaps she was a convenient target, after disagreeing with a doctor's decision?

In my mental health nursing experience many years ago, I was the subject of witch hunt after a patient alleged that a nurse had doubted the drug regime prescribed by a consultant psychiatrist. I had merely informed the patient that antidepressants don't work for everyone, an evidence-based statement, but that was enough to incur the wrath of the medical gods.

NHS management always blames nurses if something goes wrong. Doctors exert power without responsibility, while nurses are given responsibility without power. In the 1990s, I was manager of an innovative mental health crisis service. Months were spent working on the operational policy, partly to ensure that the service (which had six beds), was used for genuine crises and not as an annex to the psychiatric ward. When I objected to consultant psychiatrists transferring patients from the acute wards as overspill, senior management sided with the doctors rather than the manager running the service to the operational policy.

Instrumental to Letby's conviction was Dr Dewi Morgan, a retired paediatrician, who approached the National Crime Agency to contribute to the investigation. McLachan suggests that Evans touted for business and oversold his credentials. He was not a current expert in neonatal care, but his assessment of the cause of deaths and injuries was prominent in the prosecution and clearly influenced the jury.

Forensic analysis of the court case on the Science on Trial website rexylucyletby2023.com infers that all of the seven babies died of natural causes. There may have been clinical negligence, by doctors and nurses (including Letby). Instead, one nurse was accused of the following malice:

- Injecting air into veins (Cases A, B, D, M).
- Insulin poisoning (Cases F, I).
- Force-Fed milk. (Case G).
- Injecting air into the stomach (Cases C, I, O, P, Q).
- Attacking organs with a sharp implement. (Cases E, N, O).
- Unspecified (possible tampering or smothering, (Cases H, J, K).

Each of these allegations is undermined by the Science on Trial analysis. As well as the selective shift data, Letby was incriminated by her possession of handover sheets. Nurse and midwives often keep such records after their shift finishes, because sometimes they may need to refer to such information; for example, if an emergency arises on the next shift or next day. But these folded notes were suggested as a trophy for Letby's dastardly deeds. Also, Letby had written in her reflective journal (a record of clinical experiences kept by practitioner and used for three-yearly revalidation) that she felt somehow responsible for babies dying. Was this an admission of guilt, or simply showing human concern?

Letby was fed to the wolves, with politicians, media pundits and NHS worshippers calling for drastic action to prevent anything like this recurring. Meanwhile, there was no outcry from the same pontificators about the persistent weekly excess of two hundred deaths in Britain since the administration of Covid-19 vaccines. Earlier this year, when Andrew Bridgen was granted a debate in the House of Commons on the harm of these injections, almost every MP left the chamber.

Lucy Letby's trial and imprisonment will not repair a broken public health service. Instead, it will put more power in the hands of those who abuse it; overpaid senior managers and doctors, and a medical industrial complex that offends the very concept of patient-centred care."

Sources: wrongfulconvictionsreport.org/2023/08/28. Author: Niall McCrae (unitynewsnetwork.co.uk).

Dr Niall McCrae is an officer of the Workers of England Union and until recently, a senior lecturer in mental health nursing at King's College, London.
Norman Fenton is Professor Emeritus of Risk, at Queen Mary, University of London.
Dr Scott Mc Lachlan, is Chief Executive at Central Coast Local Health District (NSW).

EPILOGUE

"Clinicide does not occur in vacuum, it overlaps with murder by health carers such as nurses, doctors, technicians. Just as the Shipman killings were being rationalised as a once-in-a-lifetime occurrence, it was discovered that carer-assisted serial killing was on the increase. This growing phenomenon, largely directed at elderly patients and young children, is a reflection of the expanding institutionalisation of health care in an expanding and aging population. The care of children and the elderly is taken away from the family home and put into the hands of 'service providers'. Caring for vulnerable charges in a place with easy access to potent drugs, there is significant potential for a murderous carer to cause havoc. Such crimes are relatively difficult to detect and hard to prosecute.

Many of the poisons (for example, a lethal dose of potassium chloride) are hard to detect within a short time of administration. Amongst the motives given in those who were charged was 'to demonstrate the need for a paediatric care unit in a rural hospital'. Offenders have included medical, and non-medical personnel. Typically, the victims were all vulnerable, too sick, too old or too young to communicate. Researchers Stark and Paterson, have found that a minimum of thirteen health workers had murdered at least 170 patients between them in the past twenty years. Most of the cases involved nurses, many being women., (Stark, C, et al 1997). However, there were insufficient cases to build up a reliable psychological profile of the kind of care worker who could turn out to be a killer, although some had a history of previous mental health issues.

The obvious question that arises is how were suspicions of foul play aroused? Some victims survive, perpetrators were seen alone with the patient or injected medication that had not been prescribed. Syringes had been left in rooms, and drugs had gone missing. Other suspicions were raised, statistical auditing would soon reveal if something was amiss when a suspect was on duty.

What measures can be implemented to prevent clinicide? More vigilant checking of past employment records, training courses and video security surveillance as used for the detection of hospital child abuse cases, could be used to monitor suspect medical or nursing staff when on duty. Intensive monitoring of deaths is important in quiet killing settings, which should become routine practice. Health care staff need training in the detection of the 'means of death' in clinical contexts. Unfortunately, this is a woefully neglected area and requires quality controls in place to monitor unusual events. Unfortunately, one issue that will not change is expecting medical and nursing colleagues to monitor their own kind, with 'due vigilance'.

By definition, medicine and healthcare is an autonomous activity conducted primarily in 'group' settings. Most practitioners are acutely aware of the shortcomings of what they, in fact do. Over-zealousness brings its own perils, and the results are never good for medicine or society. The problems in health care and provision have encouraged a host of regulators, ranging from medical boards to health complaints units, and a flourishing civil litigation system. The prosecuting business inevitably attracts a certain type of individual, often with an ideological consumer-driven agenda. Regrettably, clinicide will continue, and it will always be discovered too late. However, some of the more sensible measures mentioned here, may result in earlier intervention."

Source: Medical Murder, Dr Robert M. Kaplan, (2010), Summersdale Publishers Ltd, (Chichester) Chapter 15, pp 223-233.

REFERENCES AND BIBLIOGRAPHY

Publications

Davies, N (1993), Murder on Ward Four, (London, Chatto and Windus).

Hallam, J (2000), Nursing the Image: Media, Culture and Professional Identity, (London, Routledge).

Kaplan, RM (2010), Medical Murder, (Summersdale Publishing, Chichester).

Morrisey, B (2003), When Women Kill: Questions of Agency and Subjectivity, (London, Routledge).

Ramsland, KM (2007) Inside the Mind of Healthcare Serial Killers: Why They Kill, (Westpoint, Connecticut, Praeger Publishers).

Journals

Stark, C et al (1997) "Nurses Who Kill: Serial Murder in Healthcare Institutions" (*Nursing Times*, Vol 93. No 3-7).

Stark, C, Paterson, B & Kidd, BN (2001) "Opportunity May Be More Important Than Profession in Serial Homicide" (*British Medical Journal*, April, 322, 993).

Thunder, JM (2003) "Quiet Killings in Medical Facilities", (*Issues in Law and Medicine*, Spring, 37. 211-37.

Yorker, RC et al (2006 "Serial Murder by Healthcare Professionals" (*Journal of Forensic Science*, November, 51, 1362-71.

"Reporting Restrictions in the Lucy Letby Case" (*Law Society Gazette*, 8 September 2023).

"The Lucy Letby Case: Lessons for Health Systems" (*The Lancet*, Vol 402, 2 September 2023).

"Letby Disaster Epitomises Flaws in the NHS", Phil Banfield, *British Medical Association, Bulletin*, 25 August 2023.)

Media Articles

"Lucy Letby found guilty of baby murders", John Pascale, (Crown Prosecution Service), 18 August 2023.

"Lucy Letby: The Nurse Who Killed", (ITV Documentary, 19 August 2023).

"Lucy Letby: The Full Story of the Serial Killer Nurse", (Channel 4, UK, 19 August 2023).

"NMC Responds to Verdict in Lucy Letby Trial", (The Nursing and Midwifery Council, 21 August 2023).

"Letby Sentencing Remarks" (PDF), judiciary.gov.uk, Manchester Crown Court, 21 August 2023).

"Operation Hummingbird: The Investigation behind the conviction of Lucy Letby" (Documentary, Cheshire Constabulary, 23 August 2023).

"What I learned about Lucy Letby after 10 months in Court", (Judith Moritz- BBC News, 24 August 2023).

"PSA Statement Responding to Calls for Regulation of NHS Managers", (Professional Standards Authority for Health and Social Care – 20, September, 2023).

"Lucy Letby Statutory Inquiry", Secretary of State Statement, 4 October 2023.

"Corporate Manslaughter Investigation at Countess of Chester Hospital," (*The Standard*, 4 October 2023. Author: Mark Dowling).

Media Sources

The Guardian
Evening Standard
Daily Mail
BBC News On-Line
Cheshire Life
Hereford Times
The Times
Health Service Journal
The Lancet
The Independent On- Line

Dr David Holding

Words Are Life's Best Selling Title

Sold world-wide to libraries, educational establishments and individuals, this is "The Pendle Witch Trials of 1612".

What it doesn't do...

Sensationalise the historic trials and associated events.

Fictionalise the already-fascinating characters involved.

Romanticise or demonise the women accused of witchcraft— or their families.

What it does...

It provides an accurate account and overview of the court proceedings of 1612, and leaves the reader to make their own decision regarding the truth behind the infamous trials.

Currently available on Amazon
Kindle £3.50 and Paperback £5.50
ISBN: 9781797806679

www.wordarelife.co.uk
wordsarelife@mail.com

Printed in Great Britain
by Amazon